Fundraising in Times of Crisis

THE CHARDON PRESS SERIES

Fundamental social change happens when people come together to organize, advocate, and create solutions to injustice. Chardon Press recognizes that communities working for social justice need tools to create and sustain healthy organizations. In an effort to support these organizations, Chardon Press produces materials on fundraising, community organizing, and organizational development. These resources are specifically designed to meet the needs of grassroots nonprofits—organizations that face the unique challenge of promoting change with limited staff, funding, and other resources. We at Chardon Press have adapted traditional techniques to the circumstances of grassroots nonprofits. Chardon Press and Jossey-Bass hope these works help people committed to social justice to build mission-driven organizations that are strong, financially secure, and effective.

Kim Klein, Series Editor

Fundraising in Times of Crisis

Kim Klein

JOSSEY-BASS
A Wiley Imprint
www.josseybass.com

Published by Jossey-Bass
A Wiley Imprint
989 Market Street, San Francisco, CA 94103-1741   www.josseybass.com

Jossey-Bass books and products are available through most bookstores. To contact Jossey-
Bass directly call our Customer Care Department within the U.S. at 800-956-7739, outside
the U.S. at 317-572-3986, or fax 317-572-4002.

Jossey-Bass also publishes its books in a variety of electronic formats. Some content that
appears in print may not be available in electronic books.

Readers should be aware that Internet websites listed in this work may have changed or
disappeared between when this work was written and when it is read.

Library of Congress Cataloging-in-Publication Data

Klein, Kim.
  Fundraising in times of crisis / Kim Klein.—1st ed.
    p. cm.—(Chardon Press series)
Includes bibliographical references and index.
  ISBN 0-7879-6917-6 (alk. paper)
  1. Fund raising—United States. 2. Financial crises—United States.
3. Nonprofit organizations—United States—Finance. I. Title.
II. Series.
  HV41.9.U5K574 2003
  658.15'224—dc22

                                        2003022255

Printed in the United States of America
FIRST EDITION
PB Printing   10 9 8 7 6 5 4 3 2 1

CONTENTS

PREFACE

Historians of the nonprofit sector will look back on the first decade of this century as a key time in the direction of the sector. For people who are interested in history, this will make fascinating reading, but for those of us doing the work and living through it, it may have more of the feel of being in a runaway truck.

I need to say up front that no one really knows for sure how to raise money in times like these. In fact, I thought of adding a subtitle, *Fundraising in Times of Crisis: My Best Guess.* Having more than a quarter-century of experience, and having worked in fundraising through a number of other difficult times—the first round of government cuts of the Reagan administration, the first Gulf War, and other recessions and expansions—and having worked around the world with thousands of grassroots organizations, I think my guess will be helpful.

This book is written primarily for people in charge of fundraising in small nonprofits (those with budgets of less than $1 million). When I use the word "you," as in "You will need to write a letter" or "You will need to identify prospects," I am speaking to development staff or executive directors. However, many small groups, especially those with budgets between $100,000 and $300,000, only have one paid staff or have a group of activist volunteers working for free. In those cases, "you" will sometimes mean a part-time staff person of no particular title, or a board member, or even a team of people who are taking responsibility for fundraising.

I suggest reading the book all the way through before beginning to apply any of the suggestions. It is a short book because people in crisis do not have time to read long books. The Resources section suggests other books that give more detailed how-to information if you need it. I am assuming you have either some experience in fundraising or access to someone who has experience. The problem in many organizations is that the experience you have—which is usually proposal writing—is not going to get you through this crisis. If you don't have grassroots fundraising experience, find people who do to be on your Crisis Task Force—a concept I detail in Chapter Three. I am not assuming you have years and years of experience, but if you do, you can read faster. Don't skip anything. Each chapter builds on the one before.

The Introduction presents the large view—what is happening in the bigger world that is affecting our nonprofit world. It is important to see your organization in the context of a large nonprofit sector not only so you don't feel alone but also so you can seek out other nonprofits and work together to address some of the sectorwide problems. Chapter One discusses why we as nonprofits are so vulnerable to the problems that emerged at the beginning of the century; one of the themes of this book is to help your organization permanently move away from that vulnerability. Chapters Two through Nine are strictly about what to do. What to do *now,* what to do in *three months,* and what to do in the *long term.* Chapter Ten discusses what the future must hold for nonprofits in order to maintain the changes recommended in the body of the book.

There are a lot of examples in the book—don't skip them just because your group is not like the one in the example. Although details have been changed, these examples are from real life. You may see your organization in the mistakes others have made or be able to avoid making those mistakes. You will also see how real groups came through some intense crises.

By the way, you do not have to be in a crisis to find this book useful. In fact, my sincere wish is that a lot of organizations will read this book and make the course corrections needed early on to avoid a crisis. It is never too early to address problems, but as you will also see, it is rarely too late. Groups of people working together can come out of some pretty deep holes.

As well as being written primarily for small nonprofits, the book is written for organizations concerned with progressive social change. These can be advocacy organizations, social service agencies, arts and culture groups, environmental organizations, libraries, or animal shelters. Philosophy, not issues, is the common denominator.

It is critical that when the history of this time is written historians will be able to say that we of the progressive nonprofit sector made decisions that raised the money we needed without betraying our mission and our goals. Let us be able to say, "We ran the good race, we fought the good fight, and we kept the faith."

Berkeley, California   Kim Klein
October 2003

ACKNOWLEDGMENTS

Above all, I thank the hundreds of organizations that have shared their adversities and triumphs with me over these past many years. I especially thank the dozens of organizations that helped me with the content of this book by providing valuable feedback, stories, and questions during the series of workshops I conducted on the topic of fundraising in times of crisis.

I also thank the excellent people at Jossey-Bass: Johanna Vondeling, acquisitions editor, who helped with the developmental editing of the book and who has been unflagging in both her enthusiasm for the topic and her insistence that the book be of the highest quality; Allison Brunner, assistant editor, who went far beyond the call of duty in getting the book ready for production on schedule; and Nan Jessup, production manager of the *Grassroots Fundraising Journal,* whose reliability, competence, and patience in keeping up with the endless details of our office allow me peace of mind when I cannot be reached while traveling or need to be home writing.

Nancy Adess, my friend and editor of twenty-plus years, did her usual job of turning my writing into an accessible and useful document. As anyone knows who reads anything I've written, Nancy is the constant in my writing that helps make what I say useful in print.

Stephanie Roth, my life partner and editor of the *Grassroots Fundraising Journal,* read and commented on the entire manuscript and originated some of the ideas presented here. She is thoughtful, thorough, and supportive and makes me laugh every day. And finally, I'm sustained by our dog, Brooklyn, her sister Gracie, who lives next door, and our cats, Jack Daniels and Ruby, who don't really care about fundraising in any time as long as they get fed and patted. They are a dose of loving reality.

—K. K.

INTRODUCTION

"The Perfect Storm"

Shortly after 9/11 I wrote an article for the *Grassroots Fundraising Journal* called "Fundraising in Uncertain Times." Now I think we have achieved some certainty about the times. This is fundraising in hard times. In fact, I believe these are crisis times—and not just because of the economy or the war on terrorism. Much has led up to the current situation, and most nonprofits are going to have to reframe their fundraising significantly in order to survive.

A crisis is not just a hard time or a cash-flow problem or a big drag. A crisis is a period characterized by a very real threat to the ability of an organization to continue its work, and if not addressed or if addressed inadequately, the crisis will threaten the very existence of the organization.

Broadly speaking, there are two kinds of crises: external and internal. The external crises we face now are changing the course of the nonprofit sector itself. To ensure that this course change is for the better will require organized work on all our parts. External issues that face the nonprofit sector as a whole include the sheer size of the sector itself, what is happening in the economy at any given time, and the attitudes and actions of current federal or state administrations toward nonprofits, including funding, regulations, and legislation.

Most nonprofits can weather problems brought on by external factors, such as the economy, or changes in funding priorities. These circumstances cause angst and cash-flow problems; they may result in the layoff of staff or the inability of the group to grow. They may feel like a crisis, and for some organizations they may create a crisis, but the sector as a whole is pretty much unaffected.

Internal crises are brought on by the action of the nonprofit itself or by accusations about some actions of the nonprofit of which the group may be innocent. Although internal crises may ripple out to the entire sector, they mostly affect the nonprofit involved in them. Internal crises include illegal activity within the organization, such as embezzlement or discrimination, or illegal activity of someone in the nonprofit, such as drunk driving or domestic violence. An internal crisis can be stimulated by a tragedy such as the untimely death of a key staff person, or a philosophical dispute that actually breaks the group in two and neither part is able to survive. An internal crisis can also be a series of small things, no one of which is particularly threatening but that added up to create a crisis. Sometimes organizations run into financial problems and not enough people in the organization are able to devote the time to raise more money, or perhaps the commitment is just not there. Some organizations seem to be slowly asphyxiated by a series of things, whereas others have one or two catastrophic and identifiable events that cause their crisis.

What makes the early part of this century different from all other times is that, starting with the downturn in the economy in 2001 and continuing to the present, we have a "perfect storm." Everything is happening at once. Every nonprofit is affected. Few will be able to grow, thousands must make serious and sometimes draconian cuts, and the very survival of hundreds of organizations is at stake.

The biggest crisis is the economy, but we cannot overlook three others: the war on terrorism, the size of the nonprofit sector itself, and the erosion of public trust in the sector brought on by scandals and perceptions of mismanagement.

THE ECONOMY

Anything that happens in the economy affects nonprofits about a year later. When the stock market started to go down in 2000, few nonprofits were affected. But the end of 2002 marked the third straight yearly decline in the Dow Jones Industrial Average and in the Standard and Poor's 500-stock index, and the effects are now being felt. This is the first time the Dow has stayed down for three years in a row since 1941 and the first time the S&P 500 has stayed down this long since 1932. This situation has a direct effect on the funding of nonprofits in a number of ways.

Foundations

Foundations are required to give away 5 percent of their assets every year. Some foundations determine that amount every year, but most elect to go with a three- or five-year average. When there are two or three bad years in the three- or five-year average, foundation giving is going to take a while to recover. For many organizations that have relied on foundation income for the majority of their funding, this is really bad news.

Interest Income

Organizations that rely on the interest from an endowment or reserve fund as part of their annual income have had to scramble to make up the recent losses from declining interest rates. This situation has particularly affected large, older institutions that tend to have large endowments.

Individual Giving

Giving by individuals is always the largest share of private sector giving and is generally recession-proof. In fact, giving by individuals has gone up in thirty-nine of the last forty years. Most experts agree that individual giving will hold steady or even increase slightly during these times. However, individual giving cannot replace government and foundation cutbacks. Individuals who give money—nearly seven out of every ten adults—are changing the way they think about giving. Some who were supporting ten or more organizations with smaller gifts are now supporting three or four with larger gifts. Others have added to their list nonprofits that are working on peace issues, or defending civil liberties, or helping rebuild Iraq and Afghanistan. As government cutbacks take a toll, many people have added or increased their gifts to their children's public school or their local homeless shelter.

While many people have actually added one or more organizations to their list, some must substitute one group for another.

Wealthy Donors. For several years, even small nonprofits were getting gifts of highly appreciated assets. However, wealthy people whose incomes are primarily derived from investments and who tend to give away highly appreciated assets are no longer able to make gifts of the size they were making. Many have had to renegotiate multiyear pledges, some have had to cancel gifts, and certainly few are in a position to take on making new or increased gifts to organizations.

High Unemployment. The employment situation varies greatly from state to state and even from town to town. Rural communities and poor neighborhoods in cities with chronically high unemployment will not notice the difference that high national unemployment makes as much as will places like San Jose or Seattle that have boom-and-bust economies. Where unemployment is a factor, nonprofits are affected. When unemployed, people obviously tend to give away less money than when they were working. With fewer employees, corporate programs that match employee donations contribute less money. Unemployed people are also not able to spend as much money going out. This particularly affects organizations that rely on ticket income, such as museums, zoos, or theaters; it also affects attendance at fundraising events. In San Jose, the heart of Silicon Valley, with tens of thousands of people out of work, the local symphony orchestra closed in 2002, and many other arts and culture groups are feeling pinched. The *New York Times* reports that large, venerable organizations such as the Metropolitan Museum of Art and the Brooklyn Academy of Music are coping with multiyear, multi-million-dollar deficits. Smaller institutions fare even worse.

Corporate Giving

Corporate giving, which is only 4 to 5 percent of all private sector giving at any time, is overall holding steady, but it is declining in places with high unemployment or corporate failures. There is also a decline in other things that corporations tend to provide, such as printing services, underwriting, sponsorship, or loaning executives as volunteers.

Government Funding

Government at all levels is cutting funding. Many state governments are in very bad financial shape and are making enormous cuts in health care, education, and social service. Organizations that had been able to count on significant government support now find themselves having to raise money from individuals. As organizations from the public sector enter the private sector to raise money, there is more competition for the donations of individual donors. Further, a very conservative philosophy continues to dominate our federal and many state and local governments. This philosophy holds that the private sector can do most things more efficiently than the public sector and that tax cuts spur the philanthropy that will be required for funding services previously funded by government.

I am not an economist and I do not know when a recession becomes a depression, but the euphemism "economic downturn" (like another euphemism, "collateral damage") hides both the scope and the nature of the problem.

THE WAR ON TERRORISM

The second factor affecting nonprofits is domestic fallout from the war on terrorism and, of course, the aftermath of the wars on Afghanistan and Iraq. These consequences are felt in a number of areas.

Immigrant Service and Advocacy Organizations

Organizations working with immigrants face a host of issues they did not face before 9/11, as immigrants confront a wave of repression not seen in years. Immigrants have been detained, sometimes for months, without being accused of anything. Some social service providers have been told to verify the citizenship of people seeking services and to deny service to anyone without proper identification. Aside from the moral issues here, in many cases this is a ludicrous request, as homeless people, women going into labor, or children may not be traveling with passports and birth certificates.

Donor Wariness

The USA PATRIOT Act (USA PATRIOT is an acronym for Uniting and Strengthening America—USA—by Providing Appropriate Tools Required to Intercept and Obstruct Terrorism—PATRIOT), passed just after 9/11 while Congress was shuttered to the public because of the anthrax scare, gave sweeping powers to law enforcement. Unknown to many people is the extent to which the PATRIOT Act, and the additions to it that have passed since then, can be used against nonprofits. The nonprofit OMB Watch (2001), which promotes government accountability and citizen participation, reported that the USA PATRIOT Act "gives the government broad powers to investigate (people and organizations) for intelligence purposes, without requiring probable cause that a crime is involved. The Attorney General or Secretary of State could designate a group as a terrorist organization and there are no procedural safeguards to protect against a wrongful designation." Several organizations working with immigrants, or critical of U.S. foreign policy, or working on various environmental issues have found themselves caught up in these "intelligence" investigations. According to Richard Moyers, director of the Ohio Association of Nonprofits, in the *Chronicle of Philanthropy* (2002), at least five Muslim charities have been shut down by the FBI; their offices locked and their assets seized. The *New York Times* (Lichtblau, 2003) reported on February 11, 2003, that in only one case was someone convicted of terrorism, when a charity leader pleaded guilty to supplying Chechnyan rebels with boots and tents.

In a discussion on February 2, 2003, about the proposed Domestic Security Enhancement Act with Chuck Lewis of the Center for Public Integrity, Bill Moyers quotes provisions of the act that would "give the Attorney General the unchecked power to deport any foreigner . . . including lawful permanent resident aliens [sic]. . . . It would give the government the power to keep certain arrests secret until an indictment is found. Never in our history have we permitted secret arrests. It would give the government power to bypass courts and grand juries in order to conduct surveillance without a judge's permission."

Consider this provision of that bill, described by Bill Moyers, from the point of view of a donor: "One of the provisions in here is that the government could actually strip citizenship from someone if you were found making a contribution to what you thought was a legitimate nonprofit organization or foundation that was later accused of being a terrorist organization."

These bills, even if they don't pass or once passed are overturned, have a chilling effect on contributors to controversial causes. Muslim charities are already reporting a decline in donations and donors, even ones that only operate in the United States and provide social services to a specific, geographically defined community.

Organizations Engaged in Research

There have been a large number of rollbacks to the Freedom of Information Act (FOIA) since 9/11; the U.S. Attorney General has instructed every federal employee that if there is *any* doubt about an FOIA request, it is to be denied (American Civil Liberties Union, 2001). Organizations that do research on environmental, public policy, or civil liberties issues are unable to get information that used to be obtained fairly routinely. One effect is that it's now harder to discover the extent to which a nonprofit or an activist may be under surveillance.

Many of these new provisions remain to be tested for constitutionality in court and they may not be uniformly enforced. But they can do a lot of damage in the meantime, in part by striking fear in the hearts of donors. There are nonprofits working to overturn these laws, and the sector as a whole is becoming more involved in educating the public about the nature of these laws. But it will take a long time to fully undue the damage that has already been done.

THE SIZE OF THE NONPROFIT SECTOR

The final element that makes this century different from earlier times is the size of the nonprofit sector. Today, as Lester Salamon points out (2002, pp. 7–8), there are nearly 1.5 million registered nonprofits in the United States;

in 1983 there were 300,000 nonprofits; in 1993 there were 750,000. To get a sense of the size of the nonprofit sector, if it were a single industry, it would be our nation's largest industry. It employs 7 percent of the workforce, making employment in nonprofits three times that of agriculture and 50 percent greater than construction, finance, insurance, or real estate. The nonprofit sector is a multi-billion-dollar arena, with a huge number of organizations competing for funding.

Scandals

With this many organizations in the sector, there are bound to be those that are run incompetently, where staff or board exercise poor judgment, and even where there is criminal activity. Because people have historically had a great deal of faith in the nonprofit sector, a scandal in the sector feels like a huge betrayal. There have been a number of well-publicized scandals recently, which has led to an erosion of public trust in nonprofits. Here are a few of the more prominent recent examples:

- The Red Cross led donors to believe their money would be used only for victims of the 9/11 disaster, when in fact some was being held in reserve for future problems.

- The Irvine Foundation was paying its outgoing executive director $700,000 in salary and benefits (more than twice as much as his more well-paid peers) while having to lay off staff.

- The Nature Conservancy was giving current and former board members unfair and possibly illegal financial advantage in land acquisition deals.

- A Goodwill Industries official was accused of skimming $800,000 from the proceeds of the stores under his management.

- A nonprofit handling some of the accounting functions for United Way of the Bay Area and United Way of Seattle closed down when it ran out of money.

These are high-profile scandals that span a gamut of large nonprofit organizations and add to the feeling that corruption can be found throughout the sector.

Giving USA's 2002 *Update* (American Association of Fund Raising Counsel Trust for Philanthropy, p. 2) notes that the Brookings Institution and the INDEPENDENT SECTOR have reported that trust in nonprofits is at an all-time low. Still, more people give away money (70 percent of households, according to the American Association of Fund Raising Counsel Trust for Philanthropy, 2003) than vote in many elections (30 to 40 percent), showing that people still have more confidence in nonprofits than in their elected officials.

It is very important, however, for nonprofits to take the public trust seriously and to make sure they do not abuse it in any way. They must be good stewards of the money entrusted to them and remember that to work for a nonprofit, as either staff or a volunteer, is to choose to be in a service profession. People who want to get rich need to choose a different sector to work in. Corruption, deception, and impropriety must not be tolerated. The vast majority of nonprofits are honest, hardworking, and effective, and are supported by the volunteer efforts of a large cross section of the public. Public trust is the sector's biggest asset. We have earned it over decades of work; a handful of scandals will not destroy it.

Mission Drift

Many nonprofits that have no taint of scandal suffer from another downfall, called mission drift—powerful economic forces move them from their original mission to other kinds of work or ways of working. Mission drift can be far more insidious than a scandal because everyone involved is trying to do the right thing.

For example, in the mid- to late-1990s, organizations were encouraged by foundations to "think big." Grants of $50,000 and $100,000 were common, and grants of $5,000 were considered very small. Even foundations and organizations that should have known better were caught up in the "glory days." As a result, many nonprofits grew at a phenomenal rate. Staff often took the place of volunteer effort. Many organizations stopped relying on volunteers altogether and lost the ability to recruit and keep them. The skill set developed for fundraising focused on getting foundation grants: proposal writing, foundation research, and building relationships with funders. Certainly these are valuable skills, but the skills of grassroots fundraising, creating and maintaining a broad base of individual donors, and developing a diversity of income sources were not developed in staff and volunteer activists in any systematic way during this time.

Now, many young nonprofit organizations and their staff have no ability to live in this new, much colder world. Dozens of these organizations have gone out of business in the last year; many more are on very shaky financial ground. The advice to "think big" was not wrong, but now we must work for new definitions of "thinking big" and thinking long term—definitions that do not require money as their main variable.

Another example of mission drift can be found in organizations that have created income streams such as fees for service and products for sale. These fundraising strategies are very important to explore and can mean a significant non-donor-driven amount of income. For many organizations, this income has kept them afloat. The danger is that services can become skewed toward those who can pay, leaving behind those who were the original constituency of the mission.

A TIME OF CRISIS

All of these factors—the economy, the war on terrorism and the concomitant war on civil liberties, and the problems that come with the size and scope of the nonprofit sector—create a time of crisis. Many organizations are already experiencing the crisis, and many more will. Few will escape unscathed, and all of us in the nonprofit sector must pull together to address some of these concerns. Lester Salamon writes in his book, *The State of Nonprofit America* (2002, p. 52), "The quality of a nation can be seen in the way it treats its least advantaged citizens. But it can also be seen in the way it treats its most valued institutions." Salamon argues that broad government support, better incentives for giving (including a tax credit rather than a tax deduction), and greater awareness on the part of the public about the role nonprofits play are required for a truly healthy sector that best serves the country.

SOCIETY CAN CHANGE

There are many specific ways to raise money during times like these; the rest of this book is devoted to explaining how to do so.

Above all, we must have faith in the power of people to make changes and the ability of a society to change. Our faith must have a multigenerational perspective. I often think about the suffragists—Elizabeth Cady Stanton, Susan B. Anthony, Sojourner Truth, and others like them—who never got to vote. Our faith must be grounded in solid planning and strategizing. Faith is not just hoping things will turn out all right. Instead, to take a page from the Bible (Hebrews 1:1), "Faith is the evidence of things not seen, the substance of things hoped for." Nonprofits are the holders of that faith in this time. We put forward a message that the environment can be saved, racism can be ended, children can grow up safe and well loved, politics can be infused with integrity, violence is not inevitable, hunger can be eradicated. We tell people, "Here's how. Here is our plan."

This book will help you plan during this time and help you get through to brighter days ahead.

CHAPTER 1

Cultural Factors
That Lead to Crisis

To fully understand the funding crises that nonprofits are facing in the first decade of the new century, one must consider two macro issues:

- A pair of endemic problems with fundraising that leave nonprofits particularly vulnerable to the current external crises as well as more likely to face internal problems
- The lack of agreement in the sector, as well as in the public, about the role of taxes in providing funding to nonprofits

The two endemic fundraising problems are large and multilayered, but can be summarized as, first, a misunderstanding of the sources of funding, which leads to compartmentalizing fundraising and looking for money in all the wrong places, and second, an inability or unwillingness to ask for money, with a concomitant lack of organization in keeping track of gifts, treating donors properly, and building a base of supporters.

SOURCES OF FUNDING

A big aspect of the first problem is simple: people in nonprofits know they need money, but they don't know where to look.

Here is what every nonprofit needs to know. There are three sources of money for all nonprofits: the government, called the public sector;

foundations, corporations, and individuals, which are collectively known as the private sector; and earned income from fees for services and products for sale. *Of these, the government in its various branches provides about 30 percent of all nonprofit income, 18 percent comes from the private sector, and a little more than 50 percent derives from earned income.*

Most small secular nonprofits, as well as almost all religious organizations, depend on the private sector for most of their money, even though many of them also have a revenue stream—which can vary from tiny to significant—from space rental, product sales, or fees.

PRIVATE SECTOR GIVING

Most people believe that foundations and corporations give away most of the money available from the private sector, and they are surprised to learn that, in fact, the majority of donated funds (on average, 85 percent) are from individuals, both living and through bequests. About 10 percent of donated funds are provided by foundations; the remaining 5 percent come from corporations. Further, INDEPENDENT SECTOR (2001)—a coalition of leading nonprofits, foundations, and corporations that works to strengthen the nonprofit sector—has shown that around 80 percent of the money given away by individuals comes from families with middle- and working-class incomes—in other words, the majority of the population gives away the majority of money. Certainly the wealthy minority account for a great deal of giving, including almost all the very large gifts, but these statistics show that an organization does not need wealthy donors to survive and grow.

The myth that most money comes from foundations and wealthy people keeps many organizations from raising money in their communities. They believe their constituents are too poor to give or that foundation funding is easier to raise than "a lot of little gifts," which is how most groups interpret the idea of an individual donor base. Many believe that individuals give primarily to their religious institution and will not support secular causes. This last belief is easy to correct: although a little less than half of all money given away does go to religious groups, just under half of all nonprofits are religious groups, which means that religious groups get exactly their share of dollars given. Furthermore, and perhaps key, people who give to religious groups are more likely to give to secular organizations than are people who have no religious affiliation.

Because of the belief that most charitable giving comes from foundations, corporations, wealthy people, or even from government, organizations that are big enough will tend to hire "development" staff who are charged with bringing in the money. This is a misplaced assignment. The job of a development director is actually to coordinate the fundraising efforts of the entire organization. In most organizations, however, instead of doing that coordination and team building, the development staff tend to be split off from the rest of the group. Development people are often not part of program staff meetings, even though they discuss programs with donors and funders and need to be as articulate as anyone else in the organization about it. Even if they are included in program meetings or planning, they are often brought in to provide information and not because their opinions are welcomed.

Development staff are sometimes even paid on a different scale than other staff, leading to misunderstanding and resentment. For example, in many organizations the development director is paid the same or more than the executive director, even if on the management chart the development director and program director are equal. Sometimes the development director is given a bonus at the end of the year even though no other staff members are rewarded this way. Sometimes they are paid on a commission, a practice highly frowned on in the field for a number of reasons. (A helpful article on this topic is "Why Good Fundraisers Are Never Paid on Commission," Klein, 2001.)

All these conditions mean that the work of the development director is measured only by how much money they bring in, even though they may have little control over all the other variables that affect fundraising and in spite of the fact that there are many other equally important measurements of development success. Especially if they are to write proposals to get grants, development staff may be spending a lot of time and organizational resources trying to raise money from a source where the money is either limited or of limited duration. On the other hand, if they are charged with building a base of individual donors with no help from board or staff, their efforts will be equally frustrating. A single development staff person does not have enough hours in the day to do all that must be done to adequately acquire and maintain a donor base.

RELUCTANCE TO ASK FOR MONEY

The second endemic fundraising problem is that even when people learn that developing a broad base of individual donors is going to raise more money over a longer period of time for their organization than seeking funds from the public sector or foundations and corporations, they run up against their deep-seated reluctance to ask for money. There are a variety of reasons for this hesitation, starting with the fact that in many cultures talking about money is taboo. Some people find asking for money demeaning. Others are afraid that if they ask someone who actually gives the organization money, then they will owe that donor a personal debt. Perhaps that person will ask them and they can't afford to give to every cause their friends are involved in. Money has been freighted with a lot of mixed meanings. For example, the saying "Money doesn't buy happiness" is often followed by the rejoinder "If you think that, you don't know where to shop." Or "The Golden Rule means that the person with the gold rules" contrasts with "You can't take it with you."

Organizations find that their fundraising efforts are hampered by volunteers' and board members' reluctance to ask for donations. Board members have actually told me that they would rather rip their fingernails off than ask for money. These people are in every other way very committed to their organization.

Over the past thirty years, there has been a lot of effort to begin to break down this taboo, but it is very difficult to rid it from the cultural psyche. Books such as Gary and Kohner's *Inspired Philanthropy* (2002), Mogil and Slepian's *We Gave Away a Fortune* (1993), and the Funding Exchange's *Robin Hood Was Right* (Collins and others, 2000) have examined the taboo about money and its relationship to classism and have provided excellent insight into how to use wealth to create social change. Suze Orman and others have helped people, particularly women, understand how to become financially secure and have helped break down the jargon that surrounds investment and capital. Amy Domini, John Harrington, and dozens of others have created the idea of social screens for investments, and the Interfaith Committee on Corporate Responsibility has made a science of shareholder activism. Dozens of fundraising trainers and programs have tried to break through the taboo about asking for money. With all this effort, progress has been made. In a room of people from twenty to sixty years old crossing class and race lines, the younger people will have a much shorter list of inhibitions about asking for money than the older people, regardless of race, class, or gender.

The Politics of the Money Taboo

The main purpose of the taboo about money is to maintain a capitalist system. If I can't ask for money, I will be shy about asking for a raise. If I can't ask someone at my workplace what they earn, or if it is "not done" to reveal my salary, I will not learn that I am paid more because I am white or less because I am a woman. When we observe children we see that our inability to ask for money is strictly learned behavior. Children have no trouble asking for money nor do they take offense when the answer is no. They believe in asking frequently—they ask more frequently than a house of worship does! As they get older, children learn that to fit into this society and take their rightful place, they must stop being so straightforward about money. However, for those of us who question "fitting in" and "taking our rightful place," we must also question the taboo about talking about money. In fact, if we won't deal with money, learn how it works and how to ask for it, we wind up collaborating with the very system our work is designed to change. Seeing our inability to ask for money in a more political context helps people overcome their anxiety about doing it.

Reluctance to Ask and Relations with Donors

Our reluctance to ask for money not only inhibits getting friends or colleagues to give, it also inhibits how we deal with current donors. Our embarrassment about asking carries over into talking with or writing to people about their giving. This hesitation, coupled with organizations pushing development directors off to themselves, contributes to the disorganization many nonprofits experience in their fundraising. Thank-you notes, newsletters, renewal letters, and annual reports go out late or not at all. Letters to donors are not personalized and the donor has no reason to think that the organization even notices his or her gift.

Let's take an example. A board member invites a friend to join an organization. The friend joins and receives a thank-you note from a staff person. In subsequent years, that donor receives a form renewal letter. The board member does not want to embarrass his friend by sending a personalized renewal letter and putting pressure on the friend to give again. From the friend's viewpoint, however, the board member does not seem to care one way or the other about whether he renews. In fact, the board member doesn't even seem to care that he gave in the first place, since the thank-you note wasn't from him!

In another example, an organization writes a compelling direct mail appeal and hundreds of people respond. But all the subsequent appeals say the same thing as the first appeal. There is no acknowledgment of the first gift and no sense of building a relationship with the donors. For other organizations the problem is that the quarterly newsletter they promised members comes out once a year! Maybe the organization meant that the newsletter would come out in some quarter.

This seeming disorganization and impersonal treatment of donors is caused by the executive director or development staff being overwhelmed along with the underwhelming involvement of volunteers in fundraising, which in turn is caused by this deep anxiety about asking for money. Consequently, organizations experience chronically high turnover in donors, with many giving once and not again, though the organization solicits them over and over. The organization then replaces them with new donors—who will be alienated the same way. Much money and goodwill are lost in this scattershot approach to fundraising.

THE ROLE OF GOVERNMENT IN FUNDING NONPROFITS

The second macro problem results from a lack of philosophical agreement among the public about the role of taxes in funding social services and cultural programs. During economic downturns, federal, state, and local governments cut funding with little consequence because a critical mass of the public does not demand that public schools, public libraries, public pools, public hospitals, or public parks and the like continue to be funded adequately with money taxed from the public.

Mirroring the public at large, people in nonprofits also fall across the spectrum of belief, from those who believe that all social services, arts, and culture should be entirely supported with taxes, that our country should have universal health care, universal education, and a guaranteed annual income, to those who favor government support to a lesser extent, and those who believe that good government is less government. Those at the "less government" end of the spectrum often feel that government is inefficient and that with lower taxes people will give away more money, mitigating the lack of government funding by private donations.

There are no hard-and-fast party lines here. Those who believe that taxes should pay for social services are also often critical of government waste and bureaucracy. Those who believe that the government should pay for as little as possible often support a strong military that uses the lion's share of tax dollars. When issues of public policy such as gun control, reproductive rights, charter schools, prisons, or environmental protection are discussed, the lines will cross and re-cross a number of times.

The nonprofit sector is as divided as the nation on these issues, and nonprofits working on public policy and tax issues debate each other and provide the research and information for the debates carried on by politicians and commentators. Taxpayers often see the issue in practical, if narrow, terms—they would usually prefer to pay lower taxes. Though they will support federal tax cuts, they will also vote for bonds to improve the schools, expand or maintain parks and wilderness areas, or create bike paths, showing that they understand the role of taxes in their local communities but may not see the benefit of paying taxes to a large federal government. Since under our regressive tax structure the people who pay the highest taxes relative to income are the middle class, those who favor greater government support of social and cultural programs are hard put to make the case that people should pay more in taxes without also calling for an overhaul of the tax system to make it more equitable.

At the same time, it is clear that private funding cannot replace government funding.

There needs to be much clearer and more constant public education about the role of taxes, the way taxes are levied, and the type of taxes we pay. For example, in states that have high sales tax but no state income tax, efforts to institute an income tax usually fail, voted down by the poor and working-class people it would most benefit, even though it can be shown that they would have more money by paying income tax and decreasing sales tax. Or, for example, Americans will generally favor lowering capital gains tax (depending on one's tax bracket, capital gains tax is for the most part lower than income tax), even though many of those same people will never pay capital gains tax and would be better off if capital gains were taxed at the same rate as income tax. Estate tax (renamed incorrectly by conservatives as the "death tax") is the most obvious of the problems in the tax debate. Our nation's oldest tax, estate tax is a redistributive tax that keeps us from becoming an aristocracy. Only 2 percent of estates will pay estate tax, yet most Americans will vote to abolish this tax altogether.

There are nonprofits whose mission is to educate people about the economy; they have often been effective. For example, United For a Fair Economy organized a speaking tour featuring Bill Gates Sr. and Chuck Collins supporting estate tax law. Hearing very wealthy people talk about the importance of estate tax is inspiring and convincing and may yet keep estate tax repeal from becoming permanent. Because of the tax benefits from giving either from income, capital, or estate, the tax debate should be of concern to fundraisers and the sector as a whole, yet historically, except for organizations specifically working on tax reform, the nonprofit sector has tended to stay out of the debate.

Unlike many Western democracies, which fund social services at a much higher rate than in the United States, we do not have a national consensus on the role of taxes. It is unlikely we ever will without a much more informed debate on this issue and a lot more education of the public. Until then, nonprofits will be at the mercy of whatever administration is in power in terms of the availability of government funding.

THE COST OF DOING BUSINESS

These macro issues are compounded by a number of smaller ones. Foremost among these, and to which a number of others are related, is the public's unrealistically low expectation of how much money nonprofits should spend on administration and fundraising.

Legitimate Administrative Costs

Donors have been taught to ask, "What percentage of my money goes to administration?" The problem is there is no simple or right answer to that question. Nor do donors necessarily know what answer would be correct. A favorite pastime of many newspapers is to expose how much money a nonprofit uses for administration. Headlines such as, "Questions Arise on the Accounting at United Way," or "Nonprofit Compensation Up," or "A New Charity Watchdog Rises," give the impression that many nonprofits do not use money wisely. A constant obsession with many nonprofits is to try to disguise the amount of their administrative overhead. Groups often ask questions like these: "If our fundraising appeal has an educational element, can we put some of the cost of it under program?" or "Do we have to show rent as an overhead cost or can we divide it among all our projects?"

Here's the real question: "How can we reclaim administration and overhead as a legitimate cost of doing business?" Take two groups (true stories, slightly disguised). Organization A has three very committed social workers providing direct service to a much-too-large case load. The social workers are compassionate and work well with clients. However, they refuse to make time to fill out forms, write reports, or deal with "all that bureaucratic crap," which is what they call anything related to paper. Their reporting failures have caused the organization to miss several grant opportunities resulting in the loss of thousands of dollars. The agency administrator works long hours piecing together the information needed for various reports and running interference with funders. Several times, she has managed to meet a deadline and save a source of funding, even though much of the reporting is not her job. The organization is now in a budget crunch, predicted months ago by the administrator and brought on by the refusal of the social workers to fill out the paperwork required by their various granting agencies. The board recommends laying off the administrator. "Cut overhead," says the chair. "Our services are more needed than ever."

Organization B has an executive director who loves "program work." He does not like fundraising or doing supervision. He has two other staff who are largely left to their own devices to figure out their work. One has figured out that he can steal upwards of $2,000 a month in forged reimbursements, petty cash, and charging office supplies to the organization's account, then reselling them to other people for cash. Discovering an inordinate amount of money being spent on office supplies, the board's treasurer suggests "cutting overhead." The office supply line item is cut in half, but it takes an audit a year (and $25,000 in stolen funds) to discover the truth. (By the way, an audit is an administrative cost.)

Of course, some nonprofits do waste money on overhead costs; the vast majority do not. Mr. or Ms. Generous Donor do not have an accurate way to figure that out, yet they are being told that finding out how much a nonprofit spends on "administration" or "overhead" is a key element. The less it spends, goes the thought, the better the group. When Ted Turner pledged $1 billion to the United Nations, he was quoted as saying that not one penny of his money was going to administration. I thought to myself, "Well, Ted, how is your stock going to be sold? Who will send you the records you need for your taxes? Without any administration, there will be no accounting for your gift." When donors are promised that "all of your gift will go to programs," this may well be true; but it will be true because 100 percent of someone else's gift is going to administration.

We must educate our donors and the general public about what makes a nonprofit honest and effective. Simply looking at percentages or amounts spent on salaries compared to other costs tells donors nothing. The nonprofit sector as a whole needs to educate the public about what questions will really get donors the information they need, but nonprofits will have to be willing to come out of the closet about the issue of administration.

Fundraising Costs

In addition to the overhead debate, the cost of fundraising raises its own set of issues. "How much should a group spend on fundraising?" is a common question, but assigning a percentage of the organization's budget will not tell you very much. There are many deeper questions and variables that have to be taken into account. For example, a brand new group may spend more on fundraising than a hundred-year-old institution. Sending direct mail appeals costs much more than administering a planned giving program, but an organization cannot start its fundraising with a planned giving program. Rarely will a donor make their first gift as a bequest. Direct mail will acquire the donors who will eventually become planned givers. A special event may raise a lot of money or raise no money and still be very successful, depending on what the organization wants to accomplish. For fundraisers, the issue of cost is a constant headache.

Disguised Costs

Related to costs is the perennial problem that the true cost of doing business for almost every nonprofit is disguised because of the assumption that everyone will work overtime without extra compensation. There is some evening and weekend work in every nonprofit. People who want a straight nine-to-five job will probably not find a home in a nonprofit. But when a person has to work three evenings a week or every weekend, something is wrong. What is amazing is that some community organizing job descriptions call for a sixty-hour week! In many offices, it is part of the office culture to work hours of overtime without compensation or time off. The problem is that a job that takes sixty hours a week to do is really one and one-half jobs. To pay only one person for all that work disguises the true cost of the function that person fulfills. When that person leaves, another may not be willing or able to work that hard. She or he will then be blamed for not getting enough work done. Many times talented staff members leave an organization because they "want to have a family." They do not see a way to have a job and have a child. This difficulty falls particularly hard on women and has been the subject of a number of workshops at community organizing conferences over the past ten years, as people in the nonprofit world try to grapple with the issue.

It is also common for an organization to "save" money by paying for few or no benefits. More than 30 percent of nonprofits do not offer health insurance to their employees, and many that do choose plans with very high copayment requirements. Only a tiny handful of plans will include dental or optical coverage. Most nonprofits do not have pension plans or child care (either at their facility or as a reimbursable expense). Consequently, there is very high turnover in nonprofits and the cost of the turnover—advertising for the job, interviewing and hiring, training the new person—is far greater than paying people decently to work a humane work week with adequate benefits and thus retain them.

FUNDRAISING, NOT COST CUTTING

Whenever there is a funding problem, the tendency of most people in nonprofits is to think about how to cut corners rather than look at the larger picture—how to raise more money. Although lack of fundraising or the failure of a fundraising plan may be seen as the problem, fundraising is rarely seen as the solution. For people in development, this translates into a job that has high responsibility and little authority. The development person is responsible for raising the money needed to run the organization but has no say in correcting the problems that may lead donors or funders not to give. The attitude of the board and executive director, which should be, "How can I help with fundraising? What should I do? Let's create a plan together," is far too often "Get more proposals out" or "How are you doing on identifying major donors?"

The issues I am describing here have been true for decades. In this decade, however, they provide an unstable foundation for all the current problems. Nonprofits that change their fundraising course in some fundamental ways that are described in this book will be strong enough and flexible enough to survive the many funding storms that swirl around them.

For many nonprofits, "fundraising in times of crisis" may be looked back on as "fundraising in times of blessing." Those who survive and thrive will make the changes we need to make and will make them permanent.

CHAPTER 2

Are You in a Crisis?

With the information in Chapters One and Two as background, we can now move to identifying your particular situation and then on to what to do. As I pointed out in my book, *Fundraising for the Long Haul* (2000, see Resources), every problem an organization has will show up in its fundraising, leading most organizations to think that fundraising is their problem. Usually, however, fundraising is a symptom of a problem or part of a larger problem. To solve the real problem requires correctly identifying it or else the solution will simply be a Band-Aid.

Further, as you analyze what is going on in your organization, remember that a problem is not a crisis. Even a serious problem may not be a crisis. To avoid a crisis, or to deal with one, requires knowing the difference.

Thinking back to the multiple-choice tests of your childhood, decide which of the following groups (A, B, C, or D), with D being all of them, is really in a crisis:

A. A community organizing group in a poor section of a big city works on issues such as lead paint in the schools and insurance companies' redlining their neighborhoods. The group has won some impressive fights and is very successful in fundraising. They receive almost every grant they apply for, and foundation funders approach them to offer grant money. Over two years, their staff grows from two members to five, then to fifteen. At that point, the activist membership becomes unhappy because only one of the staff people is from the neighborhood that the group serves. Members volunteer less, putting more burden on the staff. Concurrently, the downturn in the economy has led funders not to renew their grants. The group's income plummets as fast as it rose. The executive director lays off five people; five others stop receiving salaries and collect unemployment insurance while they continue to work. Nonetheless, the financial situation continues to deteriorate. Are they in a crisis?

B. A grassroots peace organization with one paid staff person and dozens of hard-working activists finds out that their rent is going up 250 percent. They have also racked up a number of bills, including an enormous printing bill for all the fliers and posters they have printed over the past six months. Many of their vendors are sympathetic to their cause, so have not insisted on payment, but some are asking for at least partial payment. The group is not raising money fast enough to pay their bills and this rent increase seems like a final blow. Are they in a crisis?

C. A public policy think tank with an annual budget of $400,000 has faced a $10,000 shortfall in income every quarter for the last five quarters. The first quarter this happened, the director deferred her salary; the second quarter, the director and three staff took less salary; the third quarter, the director borrowed $10,000 from a board member; the fourth quarter, the director asked a major donor for a one-time-only extra gift of $10,000. This quarter, the director is not sure what to do. Are they in a crisis?

D. All are in a crisis.

If you answered that all of these groups are in a crisis (D), I'd agree. What makes each of their situations a crisis is slightly different, but they have the following things in common:

• *No easily identifiable problem.* If an otherwise healthy organization has a serious cash-flow problem, or a serious disagreement between the board chair and the executive director, or bad publicity about something that happened, it may get into a crisis. But it probably won't, for the simple reason that the organization can focus on the single problem and, looking at all the possible solutions, solve it. It may not be easy and it may not be pleasant, but this type of situation is not a crisis. In each of the examples cited, however, a lot is going on. It is not clear what the problems are, except that there is more than one of them and they are all leading to financial problems and to pressure on fundraising.

- *No easy solution.* Each of these groups has gotten itself into hot water over a period of time, so the solution won't be a single action. Each group needs to do something quickly, but it can't be the wrong thing because they don't have the luxury of making more mistakes.

- *No going on without change.* For any of these groups to continue on their current path will result in them having to close. Each has no choice but to change, and each must determine what kind of change that will be, how fast they can change, who is going to lead the change, and above all, how the change can be permanent.

To make the point more clearly, let's look at two examples of situations that are not crises, although they need to be handled quickly.

The executive director and the treasurer of the board of a humane society come in on a Saturday to review expenses and income so the treasurer can write a report for the board meeting. They discover that their very new bookkeeper has written several $200 and $300 checks to his wife and three children. In the memo section of the account book he noted "contract labor," with no other details. It turns out that the bookkeeper is engaged in a little petty theft. In two weeks' time, he has embezzled about $1,500. He is fired and turned over to the police. As this is his first offense, he is sentenced to pay the money back and not work in bookkeeping again. When the theft is reported in the newspaper, some donors are upset. Most, however, see the situation for what it is—an unfortunate incident that ended without too much damage.

Theft is a serious crime, but in this case it was caught very quickly by an attentive treasurer. This act of theft is a drag, but it does not threaten the ability of the organization to do its job and is not a complicated problem to solve. Restoring confidence will take a little longer, but this is a one-time bad mark against the group, so it is a problem, not a crisis.

In a second example, a social service agency serving a wide range of low-income clients is told that it must verify the immigration status of the people it serves and that it is not to serve undocumented persons. If they refuse, they will lose their state funding. Since state funding contributes 30 percent of their income, the decision the group is faced with is not an easy one. Many board members see the loss of 30 percent of their funding as a crisis. However, in looking at the budget of their state and the kinds of cutbacks that are going on all around them, they realize they will quite likely lose their government funding anyway. Rather than comply with the regulation, they decide to do an organizing campaign on this issue to call it to the attention of the general public. While some people agree with the state requirement, most find it unfair and burdensome. This campaign turns out to be the beginning of a highly successful individual donor program. Moreover, because of the public pressure the campaign brought to bear on the state, the group loses only about 10 percent of its state funding. They are able to replace that funding in two years by focusing on individual donors. Best of all, they are able to stay inside their mission without diminishing their overall income.

THE DIFFERENCE BETWEEN A PROBLEM AND A CRISIS

There are two reasons that it is important to know if you are in a crisis rather than a serious cash-flow problem or a serious personnel issue. First, a crisis requires a plan that causes a fundamental shift in the way an organization does business, and this shift is a one-time-only undertaking that makes a permanent difference. A problem, like the thieving bookkeeper, may require the organization to make some changes, but it does not point to a need for fundamental change. A loss of funding, as for the social service agency, could get to be a crisis, but this organization is quickly able to regroup and launch a campaign. Although this is extra work for several people, it is less work than laying people off and reworking the program, and it yields a positive outcome.

Second, a crisis requires mobilizing help from a variety of people who will rally to the crisis but would probably not be available very often. A crisis generates a profound response to a deeply troubling situation. Everything you do to solve a crisis you could also do to solve a problem, except that it would be overkill. Donors don't like organizational crises, so you don't want to be in them very often and you don't want to exaggerate something into a crisis that is not yet there.

To know if you are in a crisis, ask yourself these questions:

1. If left unchecked, will what is happening result in our having to close our doors?

2. If left unchecked, will what is happening result in our having to change our mission significantly?

3. Do a lot of people around the organization feel that the situation is hopeless?

4. Is immediate drastic action called for?

5. Is there no clear immediate solution?

6. Is this crisis the climax of a series of events that have led up to it, even if it is precipitated by one major event?

If you answer yes to two or more of these questions, you are in a crisis. If no, read on anyway and use some of the suggestions offered here to stay out of a crisis.

Let's go back to our examples of organizations in crisis at the beginning of the chapter and identify the nature of the crisis each group was facing.

The Community Organization

The community organizing group that organized in a low-income neighborhood grew and then shrank because of foundation funding. This is a classic late-1990s organization. With lots of activist involvement from the neighborhoods they serve, this group really makes a difference in the quality of life of most people in that part of town. When the group first started, they had special events, asked for membership dues, and even had a small major donor program. They had foundation funding from the beginning, but it never accounted for more than half of their income. Paid staff and activists worked side by side. As the group attracted more foundation money, it stopped doing events. People in the neighborhood who weren't volunteers no longer gathered to celebrate victories or help identify issues. Foundation funders, rather than community members, suggested issues the group could work on, and researchers, rather than neighborhood meetings, provided information for organizing. The executive director was invited to national conferences and no longer had time to meet with local leaders. The development director wrote proposals and reports to funders, and so the newsletter was published less and less frequently. Membership dues were given up as being too hard to collect.

Now this group has lost funding, but it has also lost its greatest asset—its membership. They may well be able to recover, but they will need to recognize whom they belong to and whom they are accountable to. Because they had only one person from the neighborhood on the staff, they had no real input from the people they served. Fundraising can help solve this problem. Reinstituting membership dues and going door-to-door to collect them will let this group be reintroduced to their constituency. Holding a special event in the community will re-energize activists, and holding some town meetings will help identify issues of importance to their constituency that the group can work on. It will be a rocky road, but this group can recover and move forward if they are able to institute permanently the changes they need.

The Peace Organization

The grassroots peace organization that has been busily protesting has no fundraising plan, probably no real budget, and certainly no one monitoring their expenses and income. They may be in serious debt, but they have no real way to monitor whether they are. They must make a fundamental shift in the way they think about themselves. This is often a stage in the life of organizations that go from being run entirely by volunteers to having paid staff. However, the situation will go beyond growing pains if they don't take seriously their organizational obligations to an office and a staff person. Sometimes organizations like this don't mature—at some level they thrive on the excitement of being in a crisis. They mistake that excitement for the feeling of really getting things done while living at the edge. I have known organizations that are twenty years old and every three or four years they are in a financial crisis like this. Someone once said, "You would think after twenty years of experience they would know how to avoid these problems, but they don't have twenty years of experience—they have the same experience twenty times." The peace organization described in our example has been very active in protesting wars, introducing conflict-management strategies in schools, and providing excellent critiques of military spending. Now they also need to create a fundraising plan, a budget, and cash-flow projections, and get the activists involved in raising money as part of their program work.

The Think Tank

The public policy think tank with an annual budget of $400,000 faces a $10,000 shortfall in income this quarter, a situation they have been in every one of the last five quarters. This is the most serious crisis in many ways because of the way the director has sought to solve the cash-flow problem. At $10,000 a quarter, she is already $40,000 short for this year, plus the shortfall from one quarter from last year. As well as having cash-flow problems, having deferred her salary one quarter and borrowed $10,000 another quarter, the organization is now at least $20,000 in debt. She turned to an individual board member for help, but does not seem to be using the board as a whole to help solve the problem—or even telling them about it. It sounds as though they haven't noticed on their own, which raises the issues of the nature of their involvement, or their ability to read financial statements, or the executive director's willingness to produce accurate statements. Each of her solutions will only work once, which means she is out of solutions now and must address this problem more realistically. The big question here is why she is having so much trouble raising an additional $40,000, which, given her budget, is not that much money.

PATTERNS OF CRISIS

You can see a pattern here: serious consequences for ignoring the problem, or possibly not being able to ignore it; the problem being the result of several actions that have gone before; and the solution being both complicated and requiring almost immediate attention. You can also see some of the endemic problems identified in Chapter One. None of these groups has integrated fundraising and program. None of them sees fundraising as a key element of their work. The community organization has been encouraged to grow, grow, grow. In their haste, they have left their community behind. The activists in the peace organization don't want to be bothered with administration and fundraising when the world is coming to an end without their work, and the think tank is trying to disguise the cost of doing business but not succeeding.

Mobilizing to solve a crisis is different from working to fix a problem, so if you are going to employ all the suggestions in the next few chapters, make sure you are in a crisis or use them to stay out of a crisis.

Immediate Steps for Managing a Crisis

Once you have established that you are indeed in a crisis, there are immediate steps you must take. If, however, you are short of full crisis status but are having serious problems that you think may develop into a crisis, or you can see the "handwriting on the wall" about your government or foundation funding and know that you do not have enough income from other sources to cover cutbacks, you may want to use the suggestions here in a modified way to avert the crisis.

THE CRISIS TASK FORCE

First, establish a Crisis Task Force. This is a group of three to five people who will act as "mission control" for the next two months. Their job is of short duration but will require a fair amount of time. If the organization has staff, one of these people should be a staff person; at least one other should be a board member; and at least one other should be an "at-large" person with no other affiliation to the group except a commitment to the cause. A loyal volunteer, a friend of a friend with some expertise in fundraising, or a consultant willing to donate time will round out the task force nicely. As much as possible, the outside people should come to the task force without judgments of their own about how the group got into a crisis. They should be able to keep focused on the big picture and keep decisions from being made based on anger, resentment, or other negative (if understandable) feelings. The Crisis Task Force needs to be composed of people who are eminently trustworthy. They will need to know everything about how the crisis happened and what has been done so far. They must be able to keep information confidential, and they need to have a calm and reassuring presence. They need to believe deeply in the organization and the need for the organization to continue.

The members of the Crisis Task Force relate to the board and the rest of the staff not only through the board member or staff member who is on the task force but also through some regular reporting to the board as a whole. Because they are not an official body, they need to be clear that they make recommendations but not decisions. However, the board can give them some authority and allow them to make some decisions, which I will discuss later. In order for the members of the task force to feel their time is being well used, the organization's formal authority structure (board, executive director) needs to take the task force's recommendations very seriously and act on them in a timely manner. Because the group is in crisis, this should not be hard to arrange, as any delay tends to worsen the crisis.

Choosing the Task Force Members

Ideally, the chair of the board and the executive director put the task force together and attend the first few meetings, but it is not required that they stay on the task force. The executive director will be taking a lot of direction from the task force and the chair will be reporting about their work to the rest of the board. Obviously, if the crisis is a scandal, no one directly related to the scandal should be on the task force. Don't spend a lot of time choosing the task force members. If board and staff cannot agree among themselves who should be on it, this should be seen as part of the crisis. Among all of you, you should be able to identify three, four, or five people whom everyone trusts to do this particular job.

Other Considerations in Choosing the Task Force

If the crisis is strictly about funding cuts, the Crisis Task Force will consist of people who will focus on immediate ways of raising money and who will create a longer-term fundraising plan. If the crisis has legal elements, then one member of the task force needs to be a lawyer with nonprofit experience. If the crisis is about financial mismanagement or poor budgeting, then a bookkeeper or accountant will be helpful. The aggregate total of the skills present on this team need to add up to a group of people able to help the organization change course and save itself. Don't ask a lawyer or an accountant or a businessperson just for the sake of having one on the team. You don't want people making the crisis into something it is not. One Crisis Task Force I knew of that had a lawyer on it spent a lot of time discussing the fact that the donor who was not able to pay his pledge could be sued for the money. A pledge is legally binding, but you really don't want to sue your donors or even spend more than one second talking about this option. The lawyer's presence in this case was not helpful.

You may wish to start the team with two people and add one or two people once you are clear what kind of skills you need.

THE WORK OF THE TASK FORCE

The Crisis Task Force is not a grand jury. It is mostly concerned with what needs to be done now and what needs to be done differently in the future. It is not trying to assign blame but instead to find out what happened in order to avoid repeating the mistakes.

The Crisis Task Force meets frequently—possibly as often as weekly in the beginning—and continues for one, two, or a maximum of three months. The meetings will probably last two or three hours and there may be one or two longer, all-day meetings. In addition, the members of the task force will be making phone calls, meeting with staff and board members, and answering questions as they come in. Task force members have to be willing to make the time, which is why the commitment must be kept short.

The jobs of the Crisis Task Force are to keep the group alive during the crisis, figure out a fundraising plan and begin implementing that plan, and identify the steps needed to ensure that the crisis does not recur. Remember, the crisis is not a one-time-only unfortunate event in an otherwise smoothly functioning organization; a series of things have led up to the crisis. There can be a precipitating event, but the event alone cannot plunge the group into a crisis. Therefore, making sure that the organization doesn't lurch into another crisis will require some analysis of the history of the crisis.

In cases where the crisis necessitates dealing with the media, the Crisis Task Force will delegate this task to a subset of themselves, another small committee, or possibly a public relations consultant. If the crisis involves dealing with the Internal Revenue Service or a state revenue office, then again, it will delegate those tasks to another small committee or auditor.

INFORMATION THE TASK FORCE GATHERS

In its first meeting, the Crisis Task Force will need to begin developing the answers to a number of questions, listed here. If all of the answers to these questions aren't available at the first meeting, then one of the first jobs of the task force will be to get the missing information. The rest of this chapter discusses each of these elements; some of these questions will also be dealt with in Chapter Four.

1. Are people committed to keeping the organization going?

2. If yes to the first question, does everyone on the team have the same understanding and complete information (as far as it exists) on what happened?

3. What is the cash-flow projection for the next six months?

4. What fundraising plans are already in place?

5. What, if any, financial reserves are there, and what are the terms of using them?

6. What is the immediate financial need?

7. What are other immediate needs (such as reassure staff that their jobs are safe or figure out layoff plans, hire an interim director, negotiate paying bills late, deal with the media)?

8. What do the funders and donors know about what has happened and what do they think about it?

9. How, how often, and to whom does the Crisis Task Force communicate what it is doing?

CONSIDERING EACH QUESTION

Each of these questions is discussed more fully here.

1. *Are people committed to keeping the organization going?* This is the A-Number One question and the answer is not always obvious. The tendency of organizations is to say, "Well, of course we must keep going! What will happen to the children/trees/clients/research if we don't?" But let me be clear from the get-go: feelings of *should, must, ought* will not sustain an organization. When people on the task force hear any of those three words, an alarm should go off in their heads.

The answer to the question needs to be a resounding, passionate, unhesitating YES! When it is a lukewarm yes, an obligatory "Yes, it is our duty," a kind of "I-guess-so" yes, or when you don't have at least a handful of people willing to put in the time, including those on the task force, board members, volunteers, and staff, to address the crisis, then think again. An organization takes up a space that another organization could fill. Obviously, if the task force realizes that the organization is using up resources and giving the impression that a particular issue is being addressed or service being provided when it is not, then the task force needs to recommend that the group consider closing. More often, an organization is doing a decent job but without any passion, creativity, or enthusiasm. That group does the community a disservice to continue existing as they are.

In the rare cases where an organization does decide to fold, the task force will decide how that will happen. Should another organization be given the office furniture and the mailing list? What termination package can be given to staff? Are there debts to be paid and who will take responsibility for paying them? What will you tell the public? Deciding to close is both a difficult decision and surprisingly complicated to carry out. You will probably want to talk with a consultant who has experience in this arena.

2. *If yes to the first question, does everyone on the team have the same understanding and complete information (as far as it exists) on what happened?*

Take the time in your first meeting to lay out what happened. This information will also inform your message, covered in Chapter Four. Put three sheets of butcher paper on the wall and label the first one "Just the Facts, Ma'am" (or if you are not old enough to remember the TV show *Dragnet,* then leave off "Ma'am"). On that sheet you will write only things that you know for a fact are true. "She had probably been drinking for some time" is not a fact. "The Community Foundation will not pay the third installment on our grant no matter what we do" is one fact and one conclusion. "We have $3,000 in our checking account as of this morning" is a fact. By writing down only the facts, people are free to say whatever they want, but validation is given to facts and not snide comments or judgments. The group is collecting facts at the same time. For example, "The Community Foundation will not pay the third installment on our grant no matter what we do." Who told them this would be true, "No matter what we do"? If this came from a program officer, is this person angry? Might they reconsider when they are not so angry? Did this information come in writing? People say a lot of things when they are angry and hurt. Those things are true at the time, but they don't necessarily stay true.

Label the second sheet of paper "How Did We Get in This Mess?" and make notes about what led up to the crisis—in hindsight, what could have been done to prevent it? This information will give you data for your future plans, and also ensure that everyone on the task force understands the full complexity of the crisis.

Make sure the meeting is run fairly strictly or the tendency of the group will be to discuss the personalities around the crisis: "Why didn't he see what was happening?" "I always knew she wasn't too bright." "I heard that the board didn't even act on this until May." Statements like this are inevitable and shouldn't be censored, but in capturing what happened in order to prevent it from happening again, try to move people into an organizational analysis. For example, "The board chair will do anything to avoid a confrontation" becomes helpful when expressed like this, "The chair of the board must have demonstrated leadership ability, including the ability to face confrontation when necessary. This characteristic should be put into the job description of the board chair."

The heading for the third sheet is "What Else We Need to Know." You need to know the answers to the question "What's going on?" But as you go along, you may become aware of other things you need to know—for example, "Has the interim report been sent to the McBride Foundation, which triggers our second payment?" or "How long will it take to fix the database virus?" Finding out what you need to know will be among the first tasks of the task force after this meeting.

3. *What is the cash-flow projection for the next six months?* When I was first in fundraising, grassroots organizations that had money in the bank to pay all their bills for the next month were considered well off. To have three months' reserve was the ideal. Today, three months' back-up is often considered minimal, and many groups feel safe only if they have money either in the bank or promised to them for the next year. In crisis times, this need for security must be reconsidered. Can you stay open for a month and use that month to raise money for the next month? This is a far easier task in the short term than thinking, "We must raise enough money for the next six months."

A cash-flow projection over the next six months will show how immediately serious the situation is. At least in the beginning, approach the crisis thinking, "How can we raise the money we need?" rather than "How can we cut expenses?" If there are obvious cuts that could be made or other ways to save money, by all means, do them. You should be making any cost savings you can whether in crisis or not. But most small organizations spend so little money that looking for places to save money that don't cause cuts in basic programs is not a good use of time.

Most people's instinct is to cut expenses rather than raise money. The task force should resist this impulse as much as possible and use this crisis as a way to create new income streams. *Cutting expenses will not provide any permanent solution to your crisis, nor will it move you in a new direction as an organization.*

For example, an organization applied for a grant to fund their first full-time staff position. That role was to be filled by an activist who had helped found the group. Despite indications from the foundation that the proposal would probably be funded, it was ultimately turned down. The group concluded that they couldn't hire this person. She decided to keep her waitressing job and continue to do the work as a volunteer. When I met with the group, I had the following conversation with her:

"Are waitressing jobs easy to get in this town?"

"Yes."

"Does the organization have enough money to pay you the same amount you make as a waitress for one month?"

"Yes."

"Then, are you willing to quit your waitressing job, work here full time, and raise the money for your salary for the next month? Are you willing to try that for three or four months while you and rest of the organization raise the money it needs to offer you permanent work?"

Neither she nor the other members of the collective that run this project had ever thought in these terms. They decided to try it for one month. She used the month to solicit ten people, who each pledged $200 per month for the next six months to pay her. That $2,000 a month was more than she made as a waitress and in fact allowed the organization to provide health insurance as well as a salary. Three of the ten donors offered to continue their pledge past the six-month point and two others promised to replace themselves with other donors. She and her group now have six months to work out a fundraising plan.

As the sample shows, your cash-flow projections will also help you figure out your immediate financial need.

4. *What fundraising plans are already in place?* The cash-flow chart will show projected income, but the task force needs to review existing fundraising plans so they can decide what new strategies to add to the mix. They also need to examine the fundraising plan to make sure it is realistic and that the planning process isn't part of the problem. Many organizations set fundraising goals that they never meet; over time, this type of planning gets them into financial difficulty.

5. *What, if any, financial reserves exist?* Sometimes organizations in financial crisis have endowments or reserve funds. (These funds are different from designated funding that has been granted to the group for a specific program. Generally, you don't want to dip into such designated funding without permission of the funder.)

Fundraising Cash-Flow Projections (Sample).

	Jan	Feb	Mar	Apr	May	June	July	Aug	Sept	Oct	Nov	Dec	TOTALS
General Expense													
Staff Salaries and Overhead	(2,200)	(2,200)	(2,200)	(2,200)	(2,200)	(2,200)	(2,200)	(2,200)	(2,200)	(2,200)	(2,200)	(2,200)	(26,400)
Fundraising Strategy													
1. Direct Mail													
Income			1,500	1,000	500								3,000
Expense		(3,750)											(3,750)
2. Major Donor Campaign													
Income					4,000	6,000					8,000	5,000	23,000
Expense				(500)									(500)
3. House Parties													
Income			1,000	1,000	1,000			2,000				1,000	6,000
Expense	(250)												(250)
4. Annual Dinner													
Income						5,000	4,000		12,000	1,200			22,200
Expense (including consultant)				(500)	(1,000)	(1,000)	(2,500)	(3,500)	(1,000)				(9,500)
5. Renewal Mailing													
Income			3,000	2,000							2,500	2,000	9,500
Expense		(250)								(250)			(500)
TOTALS	(5,200)		3,300	(200)	2,300	7,800	(700)	(3,700)	8,800	(1,250)	8,300	5,800	**25,250**

One thirty-year-old organization with a budget of $1 million had $400,000 in the bank designated as a reserve fund. The group received a string of bad news in one week: they were losing their lease and would have to move, their health insurance premiums were going up 75 percent, and they were losing a government contract that provided 50 percent of their income. They had about three months before any of these events would take place. Instead of figuring out how to use that time to start raising money, the board and staff panicked. Where should they move? How much rent could they afford? Should they get new health insurance or just pay the new premium? Should they cut the program the grant was for or try to get other funding? All of these questions are the correct ones to ask, but the group members couldn't even decide on a plan to find out what they needed to know. They wasted weeks dithering like this; in six months they had moved into a financial crunch. At that point, they started making decisions, but all their decisions were about cutting costs. They laid off most of the staff and moved to a large, converted garage that belonged to a friend of a board member. A year later, they are still not fundraising adequately and they are slowly strangling to death. They refused to use any of their reserve funds to continue their work while they figured out what to do. "The reserve fund is for a rainy day," they explained to me. "Once we spend it, it is gone." I asked them, "What's your definition of rain?" All they could think of was to hang on and hunker down, as though the crisis were a tornado and what they had to do was come out after it was all over and survey the damage. Their commitment to keeping their reserve is admirable, but they need to use some of that same commitment to keeping their group alive.

Whether to go into financial reserves, especially endowment, is not a decision to enter lightly and should only be done to help with fundraising or buy time until fundraising programs start paying off. It is not a solution to a funding crisis. In the case of an endowment, an organization needs to review what access they have to the money. If the endowment was a bequest from a single donor, the terms of the donor's will may make access difficult. Most of the time, however, the board has the option to spend out of their endowment fund under certain circumstances. Reserve funds and saving accounts can be spent much more easily. However, knowing you have that money and that you could use it if you had to is so reassuring to most people that they will go to great lengths not to use it. This is healthy if it makes people raise money and do the work needed to keep the group out of a crisis or get them out of one. It is not healthy if protecting the reserve fund becomes more important than the mission of the organization, as in our example.

If you enter an aggressive fundraising program with a "sky is falling" theme and then donors find out that you had money in savings all along, they may feel angry or resentful. Laying off staff or cutting programs because you won't touch your reserve is similarly a difficult position to justify.

Think of the reserve fund as a line of credit that you can borrow from for cash-flow purposes if you can show how you will pay it back in a few months (or next year). Don't be afraid to spend it wisely, but again, see raising money as the key to getting out of this crisis. The reserve can then be used as front money for developing fundraising strategies that you may not have been using up to now.

Many groups don't have financial reserves. If that is true in your case, you may want to approach your bank to set up a line of credit. A line of credit allows you to borrow up to a certain amount and pay it back over a period of years. You don't actually take the money until you need it, and you only take what you need and pay interest on that amount. A line of credit allows you to pay for a mailing, hire a consultant temporarily, or spend money in some other way that is necessary in the short term for the long-term health of the group.

Using reserves or borrowing money are lessons we learn from business people, who often recognize the problem in a nonprofit as being one of chronic undercapitalization. In our personal lives, we understand the importance of being able to use savings or borrow money in order to send someone to college or buy a house or a car. Though we are going into debt, we have a plan for meeting that debt and the goal is worth it. We need to use the same reasoning in our organizations.

Here's an example of how one organization uses a reserve fund to get out of a crisis. A children's museum loses its third executive director in as many years. In her exit interview, she says what the previous two directors said: she has worked sixty hours a week and is tired of it. For years, this organization has disguised the cost of doing business by having an executive director who was essentially a half-time volunteer. The organization now has to consider whom to hire and for what. They realize that they can't continue losing executive directors because donors and funders are beginning to wonder what is going on, and board members are tired of going through hirings and there never being enough money. Although they are not in a crisis yet, the group forms a transition team that functions pretty much the way a crisis task force would.

The museum has a gift shop that the board has decided can only use its profits to purchase more inventory; nothing can ever be bought on credit. However, there is never enough profit to purchase the volume of inventory required to obtain deep discounts, which would give the organization more profit. If the group were to purchase one hundred children's microscopes at a time, for example, they could get each one for $7 and sell it for $21. However, they can only buy five microscopes at a time for $15 each. They often run out of microscopes on busy weekends. Their gift shop has a very slim profit margin, and some board members question whether it is worth the effort to continue it.

The museum also has $50,000 in a savings account. They decide to invest $25,000 of it in the gift shop—purchasing inventory, advertising more widely, and jazzing up their Web site. Almost immediately, the store begins to show a much better profit. More customers come, and a year later the museum has opened a second gift shop at a mall across town, which drives traffic to the museum and generates funding. They are able to pay the $25,000 back to their bank account in six months, and they have hired a new executive director and an assistant to the director.

6. *What is the immediate financial need?* In many cases, there is no immediate financial need, but the group can project that there will be one in a few months if a fundraising plan is not implemented successfully. Sometimes, however, there is an immediate problem—the group needs money to cover debts already incurred or to pay staff. The task force should figure out what the immediate financial need is and how soon it must be met.

Many times landlords and vendors are willing to work out a payment plan if they feel that you are making an honest effort to pay them in full. If the rental market is soft, a landlord may even lower rent for a month or two rather than risk losing a good tenant.

Knowing what the donors know and what they think about the crisis (see question eight) may give you a sense of who might be willing to make a one-time-only extra donation to pay the immediate need so that the organization can create a plan to move forward without carrying debt.

7. *What are other immediate needs?* Other immediate needs can include reassuring staff that their jobs are safe or figuring out layoff plans, hiring an interim director, negotiating paying bills late, and dealing with the media. An important aspect of managing these needs is to keep the staff in the information loop. In a larger organization, management staff often know what is being done to address the crisis, but a secretary, receptionist, or part-time person may not have a clue. Being in the dark, they may wonder whether they should look for another job, or whether they will be paid. These are scary questions. When people feel they are being shut out of a process, they become suspicious. Their suspicion erodes morale and adds to the rumors about what is happening, as each of them confides their fears to other workers, friends, and family. A weekly or biweekly meeting with key staff and volunteers is very important.

Make sure you always have enough money to give people at least two weeks' notice and a small severance package. If you foresee layoffs, tell people as soon as you know for sure. In an economy with high unemployment, losing a job is hard, but losing it with little notice is devastating.

In the case of executive transitions, consider hiring an interim person while you figure out what the new director's role will be. Sometimes an interim executive director takes care of a lot of unpleasant tasks to make the job more attractive to a more permanent director. They can change the way staff have been working, institute new systems, and generally do things that might not make them popular but will make the organization run more efficiently.

Here's an example. A small, suicide-prevention hotline had two long-time employees, a financial manager and an executive director. The financial manager refused to use a computer. He kept all records in a ledger, doing everything by hand. The executive director spent much of her time shopping at inventory clearances to buy office supplies cheaply or attending conferences on volunteerism. Consequently, the organization had far too many office supplies and the volunteers basically coordinated themselves because the executive director wasn't available. Both staff were paid at the minimum wage, with limited benefits. The board thought that since the staff people were honest and got the job done after a fashion, it didn't really matter that they were inefficient.

For the past several years, the organization had raised less money than it did the year before. When the executive director quit, they were barely getting by. It was clear that the organization would gradually fade out of existence if its whole way of doing business were not addressed. The board decided to hire an interim executive director while it created a strategic plan for the agency. The interim executive director immediately got rid of the excess office supplies and asked that the financial manager learn to use a computer. When the financial manager refused, the interim executive director suggested to the board that both jobs could easily be done by one person, a new executive director, and that the financial manager be offered a three-month severance package. Although there were hurt feelings, the interim executive director was able to get the organization to a point where the position of executive director would be attractive to a new person seeking a challenge.

8. *What do the funders and donors know about what has happened and what do they think about it?* Ideally, a crisis is handled internally with as few people as possible outside the organization knowing about it. The purpose is not to be secretive but to keep attention focused on the work. However, funders, major donors, key volunteers, and any others with close ties to the organization need to find out from the organization first what has happened. That way you can control rumors and get a consistent message out about the health of your organization. (See Chapter Four for more on the topic of message and damage control.)

9. *How, how often, and to whom does the task force communicate what it is doing?* In the same way that the instinct of many groups is to cut costs,

the instinct is also to maintain a veil of secrecy over everything. It is the same shrinking, hiding, hunkering down mentality. It is very important to fight that attitude—it doesn't raise money and it doesn't build a team that wants to fight for the organization.

Making sure that people feel that decisions affecting them are not being made behind their backs or without proper consultation is very important to resolving a crisis. Often, when a group finds itself in a crisis it creates several more in the process of resolving the original crisis. Oral reports are preferable for staff to written ones. Phone calls are preferable to e-mail. Creating an atmosphere where people can ask questions, offer to help, and offer their own opinions will take time but will take less time than handling the fallout and bad feelings of not doing so.

If you have regular verbal reports, and if everyone in the organization feels that their questions or concerns are welcomed and they have someone they can bring them to, then you can augment that information with written reports to board, staff, and volunteers.

Above all, focus on the present and the future. Give people ways to be involved. Don't be afraid to ask people to help—they will be pleased and flattered that you included them.

CHAPTER 4

Mission, Message, and Damage Control

Lately, I have been hearing the following types of statements from donors:

> "I have always given to the Film Festival, but this year we need to be marching in the streets, not going to the movies."
>
> "In an ideal world, we would have a ballet here in town, but right now the money needs to be used for homeless people."
>
> "Of course preserving species is important, but with children going to bed hungry, I just can't see giving money to saving birds."

These types of remarks are indicative of how, in hard times, people begin to pose false choices: we cannot go to the movies until there is world peace, we cannot have a ballet until there is no homelessness, we can't save birds until all children are well fed. They see cutting funding, cutting organizations out of their gift-giving, pulling back, as the only way to respond to the economic downturn. The more people react in this way, the more it seems they have taken some kind of sourpuss vow—they will not laugh until oppression has ended.

First, we should remember that, in fact, there is enough money for all our nonprofits. To get them all funded will require rethinking national priorities and a redistribution of wealth, but there is no shortage of money.

Once you have reminded yourself of that fact, you will pose the question that is the theme of this book: How can our organization raise the money we need? The answer is complex, but starts with clarifying your message, which is the topic of this chapter.

In the examples just cited, the film festival, ballet, and endangered species groups had failed to articulate a compelling message to their donors, and the donors felt all right about leaving them for what they perceived to be more pressing social issues. If you work with hungry children or homeless people, that may seem like a good choice, until you remind yourself that people will leave off supporting your organization, too. Consider this comment from a major donor to a fund for low-income housing: "I am not giving any money to programs for poor people in the United States anymore. The poorest person here is not nearly as poor as people in Africa." If you make a hierarchy of needs, there will always be someone more needy and some concern more pressing than yours.

In creating a message for your organization, you find what is important about what you do—you do not pose it as being more or less important than anything else. Your work is in itself important. Your organization makes the world a better place to live.

RETURN TO YOUR CASE STATEMENT

In Chapter Three, I said that the organization needs to affirm in no uncertain terms its commitment to existing. It will be helped a great deal in this effort if it has a current and complete case statement. The case statement is imperative for doing any damage control that may be required and for making sure that everyone close to the organization is using the same message in describing what happened. Perhaps most important, the case statement is the cornerstone for raising money effectively.

Organizations that operate without a clear case are at a disadvantage in raising money before they even begin. They can't state why they need the money or what they have done with money that has been given to them before. This lack of definition makes them unattractive to donors. The sidebar shows what a case statement contains in "normal" times. A case statement is a living document that board members and staff work from to create programs and policies, and it is the foundation of a strategic plan. It should be used to orient new board members and as the basis of brochures, annual reports, direct mail appeals, and foundation proposals. Too often, however, board and staff spend a long time creating the case statement and then file it away. You should make it part of everything your organization does.

A case statement should inform your work every day. Copies of the case should be present at every board and staff meeting, and it should be the basis upon which decisions are made. It should be kept up-to-date and fully reviewed at least annually for relevance and clarity. Every person closely

The Case Statement.

The case statement includes the following elements:

- A statement of mission that tells the world *why* the group exists

- A description of goals that tells *what* the organization hopes to accomplish over the long term—that is, what the organization intends to do about why it exists

- A list of specific, measurable, and time-limited objectives that tells *how* the goals will be met

- A summary of the organization's history that shows that the organization is competent and can accomplish its goals

- A description of the structure of the organization discussing board and staff roles and the types of people involved in the group (such as clients, organizers, teachers)

- A fundraising plan

- A financial statement for the previous fiscal year and a budget for the current fiscal year

---

associated with the organization should be able to repeat from memory the mission statement, the goals, and at least some of the objectives and history of the organization contained in the case statement. The fact that most people in most organizations cannot do so is what leads to some of the crises we are exploring in this book. During a crisis, a case statement becomes a combination of an oath of allegiance, a blueprint for action, and a source of inspiration for the work ahead.

So when you first find yourself in a crisis or trying to head one off, pull out your case statement. If you can't do that because you don't know where it is or you know it is inadequate, then you will have to create a new one or fix the problems with your existing one.

CREATING A MESSAGE

If you have an adequate case statement, which we will assume you do for the sake of this chapter, in a crisis you need to add an element called *Message*. The message is specific to your current situation. The Crisis Task Force poses this question: What does this organization bring to the current reality that is so critical that the organization should exist right now? To put it more baldly, many organizations are going to go out of business in the next few years. Why shouldn't yours be one of them? The Crisis Task Force should answer the question themselves and also get answers from the board and staff. Look for consistency in the message—people may have variations on a theme, but what is the theme?

A clear message doesn't mean that your fundamental mission changes or that you even change your work at all. It simply shows the world that you have read the paper, listened to the news, and you are conscious of what is happening around you. In other words, it places your work in the context of the larger world.

Here's an example. An affordable housing group believes people should be able to live in the community in which they work, if they desire. When their organization began, their community had low unemployment, but a lot of people commuted from nearby towns because local housing was so expensive. Two years later, the community has high unemployment and people who live there are losing their homes because they can't pay their rent or mortgage. The affordable housing organization maintains the same mission, "People should be able to live where they work," but now they institute other actions to fulfill it. For example, to help people stay in their homes, they create an emergency loan fund where people can borrow money easily for housing costs, and they work with local banks to stop foreclosures. Their message is, "We make sure that losing your job does not mean losing your home." Their mission is the same, but the message reflects what is happening with housing in their community. It also reflects some very hard work on the part of the board and staff to create these new programs.

Underlining all of my recommendations about developing your message is my firm conviction that you are always best off telling the truth and only the truth. However, you may not be telling the whole truth right away until you are sure that you know the whole truth. In big crises, truth has a way of changing with time and with who is doing the telling.

When Message Is Damage Control

When an organization is in an internal crisis, the message is more along the lines of damage control — explaining what happened and making sure everyone who should has the information they need.

Here's an example. An organization has a history with sloppily kept or nonexistent donor records. Gifts are often not recorded properly, people are not thanked or they are thanked for the wrong thing, donors are reminded of pledges they have not made. A new development director has been hired to improve the situation and the message has gone out to board members that these problems are over. Early in the new development director's tenure, however, a number of events cause the board to question whether record keeping has actually improved. First, a major donor tells a board member that his pledge form commits him to a $10,000 gift when he only pledged $5,000. The executive director speaks to all parties; though the development director insists the pledge was recorded correctly, the donor is equally sure it is in error. The executive director changes the pledge form, reassures the development director that this donor has been inconsistent in the past, and lets the board member know this was probably not a record-keeping issue. Next, the development director seriously overstates the return on a direct mail appeal. When the discrepancy surfaces, he claims that his math was faulty because he was so busy entering respondents into the database that he figured the percentage of response in his head. The third month, the development director announces an impending grant for $25,000. When the executive director calls to thank the foundation funder, she learns no such grant has been proposed nor is one forthcoming.

Now the executive director realizes that the previous problem of bad systems has been overshadowed with a bigger current problem: the development director is a liar. She fires him immediately and calls the board chair, who informs the board members of what has happened. The executive director talks to the other two staff. They and the board chair agree what the message will be: "We were unable to get accurate information from the development office. Since the development director was still on probation, we have terminated his contract." The board members and the staff will know more specifics, but no one else needs to.

The executive director lets the foundation funder know that the development director has been terminated because he sometimes gave misleading information; she asks the funder to pass the information to anyone who needs to know. This funder is a reliable and trusted member of the funding community and likes this group. Her word among funders and major donors that things are being handled properly is important.

This organization averted a more serious crisis by handling the situation immediately once they understood it. In this crisis, only a few people really needed to be involved, but they were kept informed all the way. By enlisting a trusted messenger (the foundation funder), the organization was able to control any fallout from what the development director had done.

Getting the Board on Board

In crises, we often focus on the opinions of people outside the group—the donors, the clients, even the general public. Yet our greatest difficulty in forming a message and relaying it is often at the board or staff level. It is critical that board and staff feel their opinions and feelings are welcome; further, they must not feel that they are being asked to lie or be evasive with others. Board and staff must be involved in the process of exploring options and discussing all the points of view, or they can quickly feel stifled. In one such situation, the board chair explained to a major donor, "I'll tell you what I am supposed to say and leave you to read between the lines." His explanation was lost, as the message "I leave you to read between the lines" became what was told about the situation. As one funder reported to a small group, "Even the board chair just says, 'read between the lines.'" Needless to say this is not good message development.

Your message should not be evasive or vague. If there are legal issues involved, ask your lawyer what you can say and what would be legally dangerous or off limits. But if there are no legal issues, then figure out how you can tell the whole truth but keep returning to the mission of the group. Message development may take some time and may surface some important discussions as the crisis develops and is worked through. The process of developing the message can also be part of the message, particularly when some of the board members have divergent opinions, as in the following examples.

An after school program for teenagers provides a basketball court, a bank of computers for doing homework, an art room, and volunteer adult counselors. Half the funding for the program comes from the local department of parks and recreation and the other half from the business community and a cross section of parents. The program has one paid staff person and fifty volunteers; its budget is $150,000.

The park and rec department is forced to make serious budget cuts in their programs, resulting in a cut of $50,000 of their grant of $75,000 to the after-school program. Because of the economic downturn the town is experiencing, some businesses also cut back on their donations to the program. In a matter of a few months, the organization experiences a 40 percent decrease in funding.

The board calculates that they can run the program at its current level for six months while they figure out how to raise more money. They announce to the parents and students, "Everything is fine right now. We are seeking other sources of funding and we encourage each of you to give money and help raise money."

As the board works with the executive director to create a fundraising plan, philosophical differences develop. Many board members worked hard to advocate for government funding for the program. The mission of the organization, "Teenagers are a community asset and need to be nurtured," implies that the government has a role. These board members feel that even if the program could be sustained with private donations, it shouldn't be. It would be more principled to close it. "That's not fair to the kids," says the other faction. "We have to try to run the program on less money or raise money elsewhere." The board is further split when one member suggests renting part of the space to armed services recruiters, supporting the view that armed services represent good jobs and scholarships for kids along with the option of income for the program. Long-time peace activists in the group are appalled at the potential sell-out. Two months pass, with each faction getting more firmly into position and no money being raised nor any plan formed for cutting expenses. The message "We are exploring options" is wearing thin, particularly as the various arguments begin to be put forward to the parents, students, and business community. Everyone has an opinion.

The board decides on a bold course: get community input on the various options. The board writes a short letter to parents, teachers, business people, and the community at large presenting the dilemma: "How do we best show how much our teenagers mean to us? We believe our program deserves government funding, but in these times, that kind of funding is not available. If we are to replace our lost grant, we must have the help of the entire community. We need to know your opinions. Please come to a town meeting on March 23 at the Center. The meeting will start at 6 P.M. sharp with a light dinner. Bring your opinions and an open heart for listening and hearing others."

About fifty people come and meet for four hours. At the end, consensus has been reached: the program will seek private funding, but the city council will be asked to pass a resolution declaring the program a city treasure. Seeking government funding will be a top priority. The center will not be opened to armed services or any other recruiters. As has always been true, employers can post job announcements there and anyone can post announcements of scholarships, internships, and volunteer or job opportunities.

The message created at the meeting is simple, "We have chosen to put the teenagers ahead of all other concerns. We believe teenagers are a community asset and we as a community pledge to keep this program open." By going public with their differences, this organization ensured that differences of opinion about the future of the center could be reviewed in one place at one time so that they could be resolved.

Let's look at another example in which the board had to overcome differing points of view. This situation turned out differently, but in its own way, turned out well.

The founding executive director of an organization advocating for the civil rights of gays, lesbians, bisexuals, and transgendered people (GLBT) died suddenly. She had been a dedicated and articulate advocate and had devoted her life to the cause. She had spoken to every church, synagogue, service club, chamber of commerce, women's group, conference, or gathering in her state that she could. She taught a course at the local community college on counseling in the GLBT community. A small inheritance had allowed her to work without salary.

The group has two paid staff people. One was the executive director's personal assistant who handled correspondence, phone calls, and speaking arrangements; the other handled the finances, both helping to raise money and to record how money was spent.

The staff and board are in shock at the executive director's death. They have done nothing but support her since the day she started the organization. They have never taken leadership roles or proposed their own ideas. Her vision was their vision. Without her, there is, at least temporarily, no viable organization. Now the board has to figure out what the organization is without her. The board chair calls together the board, staff, and some other volunteers, all of whom were long-time friends of the executive director. Calls are still coming in to book a speaker, letters and e-mails need to be answered, and there is an upsurge in donations to honor the executive director's memory.

The board chair hires a group of organizational development consultants to help figure out what to do. After listening to them for a while, she outlines their choices:

1. Close down. Admit the organization was really all the wonderful work of one person and now that person is gone. You still will have made an extraordinary difference in thousands of people's lives. Ending does not mean failure.

2. Find another organization with similar goals and become a program of theirs. Give that group the list of your donors and what money remains in the bank account, and refer all calls and letters to them.

3. Hire a new director and reinvent the organization. Raise the money to pay an executive director, keep the two staff, and keep the program going or create new programs.

The consultants say that first the people left in the organization must recommit themselves to their mission: "We believe all things created by God are good, including all sexual identities. We imagine a world free of prejudice and stereotype and work for full inclusion in all daily life of the GLBT community."

Everyone agrees this is important work, but one by one each board member explains their position. Says one, "I mostly did this work for her." And another, "When she was here, there wasn't much work to do—just support her." Others use words to the effect of, "I don't have the energy, or time, or patience, or knowledge to recreate this group without her." One or two board members say that they think most of the work is done. Things are very different than when the group started—there are more groups doing advocacy work and people have far different attitudes than they did fifteen years ago. It is quickly clear that no one has the energy to continue the organization. A board committee finds another organization to give everything to and the group closes up the office. A letter goes out over the signature of the board chair explaining that, with the death of the founder, the time has come to let another organization carry the work forward. He names the organization they have found and asks that donors give money there from now on. With little more fanfare than that, the group closes.

There are some groups that are really the vision and the work of one person and without that person there is no group. As the consultant pointed out, ending is not failure; sometimes closing the group is the most mission-driven decision.

DELIVERING THE MESSAGE

The process of creating a message cannot be separated from the whole process of creating a response to the crisis. However, groups usually cannot wait until a full response is put in place before putting forth some kind of message. Donors, staff, and the public will need information about what is going on with the organization. The message that you start with, then, is the least amount of truth you can say without appearing to be hiding something. In fact, part of the message can be that you will be sending out more information as it becomes available. Don't be nervous about admitting that you don't know everything yet. It is better to have "not knowing" be part of the message than to say something that later turns out to be false and have to issue a correction. Further, the message cannot be separated from the messenger. Finding well-respected and trustworthy people to help you deliver your message is just as important as the message itself. They can deliver the message and then conclude (assuming they feel this way) "I think everything will be fine" or "I have a lot of confidence in the team of people who are working on this."

Make a list of the people who need to hear about the crisis first. In addition to board and staff, think about anyone who thinks of themselves as close to your organization—the organizational "family." This list will include active volunteers, long-time funders, long-time major donors, and sometimes former staff and board. In choosing whom to tell first, you don't want to create such a long list that time you should be spending on planning is spent calling people. At the same time, these close-in people are often the people you will be approaching for donations. Remember, you can always tell someone what's happening, but you can't "un-tell" them. When in doubt about telling someone, wait.

For example, an organization got into a crisis in part because of actions of the executive director, who has now been fired. The crisis team debates whether to tell the founding executive director, who disliked her successor and felt bitter that she, a founder, was not more sought out for her opinion after leaving the organization. Normally, a founding director would be one of the first to know about any problem, as that person will be called by others as word leaks out. Moreover, the crisis team considers that she will be further embittered if she learns that other people were informed before her, and it is quite possible that someone will tell her. On the other hand, they fear she may use the opportunity to criticize the board for hiring this person who has now had to be fired. She tends to be a gossip and is not well liked. In the end, they decide more damage can be done by not telling her than by telling her. She has already been so critical of the new director and the board that further criticism from her will not be damaging.

Next you have to figure out how people should be getting the message and from whom. Generally, the people who are told are told through a call or visit. Avoid e-mail, which can be forwarded too easily and may take on a life of its own. Long-time donors, funders, and volunteers make great messengers. Board members, particularly the chair of the board, can deliver the message, but may be perceived as too close to the situation, possibly involved in creating the problem, and too defensive. Major donors are usually told by the people who have solicited gifts from them in the past. The people who are told first can be enlisted to tell others. Since they will probably want to tell someone anyway, this provides some control over message delivery.

Institute a regular way to keep the people on the list updated about what is happening. If, as in many crises, the situation unfolds for a while, create a phone tree to keep people up-to-date. You can at this point decide to do an e-mail newsletter, but again, remember that anything you write on e-mail can wind up anywhere—at the office of the FBI, on the front page of the paper, at the e-mail address of the person you have fired. E-mail needs to be thought of as public information and no amount of marking it "Confidential" will really change that.

TALKING WITH MAJOR DONORS ABOUT THE CRISIS

All donors are important for three reasons: they chose to give to your organization when they could have chosen any number of others, any amount they give is that much less left to raise, and no matter what size of gift they start with, they may be able to give bigger gifts over time. Many donors who started out by giving $35 to a mail appeal or $25 to attend your annual auction later become $2,500 or $5,000 donors. A $25 donor may bring in her good friend who gives you $10,000. Further, someone who makes minimum wage and gives your organization $35 is giving almost a day's take-home pay, whereas someone who earns $100,000 would need to give about $400 to make an equivalent gift. Thus, we respect every donation.

However, major donors get more fundraising time because they are giving more money. They usually feel a bigger investment in the organization than a smaller donor does, and a few extra major gifts from them will be a big help in getting an organization through a crisis.

In a crisis, major donors need attention and reassurance. When an organization is in a crisis, the donors who agree to talk with you, even on the phone, mostly need reassurance that their gift is not going to go down the drain. Will you raise the money you need? Will you be back next year with yet another crisis? Do you really know what you are doing, and if you do, how did you get into this mess in the first place?

Most donors realize, even if they are not able to articulate it, that a crisis is not just a big problem in an otherwise smoothly functioning organization. While what caused the crisis may not be your fault, as in previous examples, nevertheless, as indicated in Chapters Two and Three, a crisis has a longer history than the crisis event. Remember also that these donors are likely being approached by other organizations that are also in crisis; moreover, they are reading about scandals, funding cutbacks, closures, and the like every day. In general, in a time of crisis, donors become insecure. They may tend to hold back or cut back, and they need more hand-holding and reassurance than they normally would.

There are four things that will reassure almost all major donors; most of them need just one or two of these elements. The four elements are an explanation, a plan, evidence of other donors, and an escape clause.

An explanation. Major donors, particularly long-time major donors, are like family. In a family, when someone has a heart attack, or a couple decide to separate, or someone loses a job, the relatives expect more information about the situation than a neighbor does. Tell these donors whatever you have agreed can be told to anyone close to the organization. Major donors will usually know about as much as any funder or board member. Don't feel you have to launch into a long explanation. Let the donor ask you what he or she wants to know after you give a brief summary of what happened. Be open to their questions. Some people will be far more curious than others; you don't want to bore people with details they are not interested in, but neither do you want to appear secretive.

A fundraising plan. A fundraising plan is a great reassurance for everybody because it shows that you have thought through what is going to be required in the next few months to move out of the crisis. Your plan should be as realistic as possible, but reality is also shaped by plans, so your plan needs to be hopeful and optimistic. Be prepared to show the donor your cash-flow chart and a strategy-by-strategy description, including gross and net incomes for each strategy. Show them your gift-range chart and talk about how many other prospects you have.

Help from other donors. Evidence that other people have bought into this plan is important. As you get gifts, ask if you can share the donor's name and size of gift with other prospects. If a donor knows that Manuel has given $5,000 and Sydney has given $2,500, and the donor likes and respects those two people, he is more likely to make his gift. Some donors are reluctant to have their names used and some are reluctant to reveal the amount of their gift. That is their privilege. You can always tell a prospect, "We have two other people who have given $10,000," without using their

Fundraising in Times of Crisis

names. Having a board that has bought into the plan is critical here. Even if the board members are not able to be major donors themselves, you need to be able to say, "100 percent of our board members have made a gift that is significant for them to demonstrate their faith in our future."

An escape plan. Some donors need to be offered a contingency—they will give only if certain things happen. Of course, such a way out should only be offered if the person clearly indicates that's what they need. If an organization seems to be telling the truth about what happened, has a reasonable fundraising plan that shows that the crisis will not happen again, and has commitment from the board and some other donors, most people do not require this fourth element.

Nonetheless, some of your biggest donors may want it. What does an escape plan look like in fundraising? Let's say you approach someone for a lead gift of $10,000 on a $100,000 goal. The person is committed to your organization but hesitates, asking a lot of questions about where the other $90,000 is going to come from. Ask the person where you would have to be toward the goal of $100,000 for them to feel that the campaign was going to succeed. Some people will say, "If you had half of it, I would feel better." Some people will say, "If you are able to get one more big gift, I would feel better." Offer the person the option of pledging conditionally. "Would you give $10,000 when we get to $50,000? Can we tell people that we have a challenge of this sort?" Some people want to see the rest of the money in place before they give their money. Offer that person the option of giving the last $10,000: "I understand your worry that we may not be able to find the rest of the money we need. We have a plan, but plans don't always succeed. What if you committed $10,000 to be given when we have raised $90,000?"

A challenge gift is a great motivator for the major donor committee to get out there. Sometimes the challenge is not about the amount of money but about who is giving it. "I'd feel better if I knew Fred was in. He is so smart about these things." You would then say, "How about if we get back to you after we have talked with Fred?" Go even further and say, "Can we tell Fred you said this? I think he would be flattered." When you go to Fred, you can truthfully tell him that his leadership gift will lead to at least one more gift. Obviously, if Fred doesn't give, the prospect doesn't have to give.

Some people want to give some money now and some later. They give an amount now because they know you need it, but it is less than they can afford to give and they wait to make sure you can raise more from other people. Consequently, one or two people may make both your first and last gifts.

WHEN THE CRISIS IS CAUSED BY A FINANCIAL SCANDAL

Simply getting more donors will not be that reassuring to someone who is wondering how your executive director managed to skim off $75,000 over three years without anyone noticing. That the treasurer of the board knew about and tried to deal with it quietly will not be helpful news. Or someone may wonder how anyone can ever trust an organization's veracity or judgment when it turns out that a program person filed a false report on progress with a foundation—a report that was signed by both the executive director and board chair. Those people's protestations that they didn't have time to read the report do not make anyone feel better. In both cases, when an enterprising young reporter scoops these stories for the local paper, they become the talk of the town (or that part of town that cares about these organizations).

Scandals are difficult to deal with because they break trust. Now the question is not whether your plan will succeed but whether you really can fix an organization that has allowed such behavior. Going back to the message, you will want to identify people who can say that they think the organization can be trusted again and the problems are being dealt with responsibly. Talk with those people. What would they need to see in the organization to feel confident about saying good things about it or putting their own money into it?

In a scandal, finding out the context of the problem often goes a long way to reassuring people that the problem can be solved. For example, the executive director who skimmed off $75,000 over three years has worked in the organization for twelve years. Five years ago, he went to a casino for the first time and really enjoyed gambling. He very quickly became a compulsive gambler and has since incurred gambling debt. The treasurer of the board and one other staff person knew the director was stealing, but tried to deal with him quietly so as not to embarrass him. The director has now been fired and is in a recovery program. The organization has learned a lesson in how to deal with painful situations and has even allowed a consultant to write up their situation as a case study and cautionary tale for other organizations. While context does not excuse anyone, knowing it does allow for more compassion.

In the second scenario, context is even more important. The newspaper story rightly said that a staff person filed a false report. But what was the nature of the falsification? The staff person lied about the progress the organization was making on creating an earned-income venture. She claimed that a business plan was almost complete and they were ready to hire a staff person when those accomplishments were at least six months in the future. The executive director signed the false report—and the board chair went along—because he thought the project delays might cause the funder not to pay the second half of the grant. The executive director should have gone to the funder and told them the project is behind. This will not be the first time they have heard that! Instead, he tried to operate in secret and the newspaper reported the organization was lying when in fact the error was very bad judgment. When the program officer of the foundation finds out what has really happened, she gives an extension on the grant and pays for the executive director to get executive coaching to help him make better decisions in the future.

In a scandal, donors need to know that the circumstances that allowed the scandal no longer exist and that the organization is thoroughly evaluating itself to ensure that nothing else is amiss. Most people know that families, businesses, and nonprofits can make terrible mistakes, but that doesn't mean everything they do or stand for is a mistake. The issue is how to put the mistake behind you without simply covering it up.

From a fundraising viewpoint, a scandal is very hard to deal with and will require even more reaching out than other kinds of crises. Tell the truth, and tell it to people whom other people look to and trust.

In the end, donors are your friends, and major donors are your family. They may not like what you do, but they will generally stand by you if they have enough history with you to know that this scandal is something you did—and not something you are.

EVERYTHING COMES BACK TO MISSION

Creating a message during a crisis is actually relatively simple once the organization recommits itself to its mission. Program or fundraising direction may have to change because of the crisis, but that step is possible as long as a group of people care deeply about the organization. If you see telling the truth as the only option, that limits what you can say. You are not going to make something up or pretend something is true that is not. You are simply going to figure out who needs to hear the truth from whom, and when they need to hear it.

CHAPTER 5

Successful Fundraising During and After a Crisis

Nonprofits in crisis have a hard time stepping back and reframing their fundraising programs. However, the reframing described in this chapter—which is to make uncertainty a part of your program—is the first step to getting out of the crisis permanently. Uncertainty these days is an irreducible part of the picture. An economic recession makes fundraising much harder because the crisis you are experiencing may be related to factors that are bigger than your organization, and whatever you do, you probably cannot change the course of the economy. However, a nonprofit that cannot survive the ups and downs of the economy is one that is in serious need of an overhaul.

Part of the reason nonprofits have a hard time creating a fundraising program that works is that they try to control the uncertainty factor—they try to have less uncertainty by planning. They create plans and then they experience the old joke, "Life is what happens while you are making plans." The paradigm we must use instead is to plan for and with uncertainty. Uncertainty becomes part of the fundraising program. As in certain martial arts, the energy of the attacker is what is used to overthrow the attacker.

There are two elements that can incorporate uncertainty into your fundraising program: diversity and flexibility. Your organization's fundraising program may have some elements of each of these, but if you are in a crisis now or anticipating one, you will need to greatly expand the ways these elements are built into your work.

DIVERSITY

For decades, the most successful fundraising programs have been built around the concept of diversity. In a recession or an internal funding crisis, groups need to return to this concept and really put it to work. Everyone gives lip service to it, but few actually implement it.

Diversity means that your organization has the money it needs coming from as many sources as it can manage, raised by as many people as you can coordinate. Most organizations get into trouble because they have only two or three sources of funding or because they have only two or three people really involved in raising money. If any one of the sources or any of the people goes away, the organization is in trouble.

Analyze your sources of funding and your fundraising team through this lens by asking the following questions:

- Do our financial sources and human resources have the capacity to grow (financial sources in terms of amount of money raised; human resources in terms of learning new skills as well as bringing in new people)?

- Can the same number of people working the same amount of time raise more money next year?

- Does any one person or funding source account for more than 20 percent of our total funding? Does any one person account for more than 20 percent of our total fundraising effort?

- Are at least some of our sources recession-proof? In other words, how important are external circumstances to the safety of each funding source?

- Do we have a strong team of people, with most of them volunteers, helping to raise our money?

- Does that team have a built-in transition plan so that as one member leaves, another is seamlessly brought on?

When you examine your funding sources and the people raising money using these questions, you can see the relative strength of each type of source. The first thing that you may see is that foundation funding is not a strong source of funding. Foundations will give money for a few years, but their grants tend to shrink rather than grow, and there are a limited number of foundations, particularly those that are interested in your work—no matter what your work is. When foundation assets shrink, their giving shrinks. When the issue you are working on is no longer in style, foundation giving also goes down, so that even during an economic boom organizations should not rely on foundations for core support.

You also see that government funding is not a strong source of funding. It is deeply affected by recessions—and also by elections. Many of us believe that the government should take a far more active role in funding nonprofits, particularly those working in the areas of health, human services, education, and the arts, but our philosophical beliefs cannot be part of our fundraising plan unless we have decided that working for adequate government funding is part of the mission of our organization.

Because of these conditions, ideally, not more than 20 to 30 percent of your funding would ever come from foundations and government sources. Some organizations are even electing to seek a smaller percentage—10 to 15 percent from these sources, using government and foundation funding for special programs and expansion but not for core program and operating income.

If you have been able to raise money from corporations, it is very unlikely to have been more than 10 to 20 percent of your total budget. Corporations tend to keep giving money to the same organizations year in and year out if they are able. If you have corporate funding, keep getting it if you can, but if you have never received it, use your fundraising time on other strategies first.

There are two income streams that lend themselves to growth and expansion, that can be volunteer-driven, and through which income can grow predictably. They are individual donors and earned income. Within these income streams are an enormous variety of options, many of which I discuss throughout the rest of this book.

What you need to do now—during your crisis or to forestall one—is to look at your sources of funding and see which ones can be expanded using mostly volunteer energy or little front money. You also need to think about what strategies with similar criteria you want to add to your fundraising plan. You might as well add them now. The temptation is to wait until you have more money, or things settle down, or you get new board members, but no time is ever exactly right to start a new strategy. Start now.

There may be strategies that you need to find out more about, particularly the strategy of earned income. Whom can you ask? What can you read? Build into your immediate plan finding out what you need to know for longer-range fundraising.

The other half of the diversity equation is people. Again, one person should not be raising more than 20 percent of your budget. A variety of people should be involved in fundraising, with new people constantly being trained and given practice so that leadership succession is built into the fundraising work. Work with volunteers the way you should be working with donors—keep asking them to do more, keep listening to them and incorporating their ideas and responses, keep finding out what they like to do and what they don't, what skills they have, and make sure they know you appreciate their efforts. Just as donors don't like to be contacted only when you want more money, volunteers don't like to be contacted only when you want to raise money. For those organizations large enough to have several staff people, figure out how to integrate program work with fundraising so that all the staff are involved in both program and fundraising.

FLEXIBILITY

The key to staying out of a crisis is to have plans that are flexible. You want plans that can easily be changed if external circumstances require. For example, a small town that has just learned that one of its most beloved young people has been killed in the war on Iraq is unlikely to turn out for a gala event the same day as the funeral—or even for a while afterward. The event will need to be rescheduled. Or the chair of your fall membership drive calls to say that he is volunteering his nursing skills at a hospital in Afghanistan so the membership drive will have to occur earlier if he is to fulfill his responsibility to it before he leaves.

We have always tried to plan around snow and rain; many of us have learned how to cope with earthquakes, hurricanes, or tornadoes; now we must plan around war and terrorism as well. Our attention span right now is exceptionally short. Fortunately, volunteer management experts have observed for the last decade or so that volunteers would rather put in long hours for a short time than dedicate a few hours over several months. Asking someone to volunteer for two or three weeks is far more likely to be successful than asking them to volunteer for a campaign that runs over six months or a year. Structure your annual fundraising into modules that last one to twelve weeks. Nothing in your annual campaign, except perhaps your signature event, ever takes more than twelve weeks from beginning to end. Instead of having one major donor campaign a year, for example, you may have two short ones—one to renew current major donors and one to bring in new donors. Or you may decide to do a marathon five-week major donor drive with something going on every day.

For development staff, this flexibility means that at any given time you only have two campaigns going. You are not trying to keep twenty balls in the air. Even when you have three grant deadlines, a membership drive and a renewal mailing with phone follow-up, as well as the usual volume of data entry and thank-you notes, you know that this period of activity is not going to last that long. The membership drive is over in two weeks and the phone follow-up to the mailing is taking place over three evenings.

For board members and volunteers, this flexibility means that you don't have to worry about how much you hate fundraising. You just do your share for three weeks and then it is over. You can find something you feel comfortable doing and some period of time that is convenient for you. When you are not working on fundraising, you know that other people are.

HIGH-TOUCH FUNDRAISING

Fundraising in times of crisis should be what we call *high-touch*. A donor's experience of giving away money must be positive in order for them to want to repeat it. With scandals causing donors to wonder if their gift was properly used or made any difference, alienation from the political process causing people not to vote and not to participate in the civil society, and economic uncertainty leaving people worrying about their financial security, what will cause donors to feel positive about giving is for fundraising to be high-touch. The donor needs to feel that he or she is supporting useful work and that the donor's gift is important to making that work succeed.

Because of the all the uncertainty described in earlier chapters, donors are thinking more about their giving than they may have in the past and are making changes in their giving patterns. Some are adding gifts to organizations addressing current pressing issues: organizations working for civil liberties and peace organizations report increased membership, and international relief groups are also raising more money. For many donors, adding one organization means taking another off their giving list. You don't want yours to be that group.

People are also looking more closely at organizations; they want to know their money is appreciated and well spent. Listing a donor's name in your newsletter is a form of personal recognition that many donors like, but it will not take the place of a personal note on your next request for money. Merely listing a donor's name in an annual report will not accomplish enough personal recognition or attention if you are sending that same donor "Dear Friend" request letters and photocopied thank-you notes. In times of crisis, donors are not as interested in public recognition and premiums, which may seem wasteful, as they are in effective programs. How can they learn how effective your work is? You will have to tell them, and tell them as personally as possible. In times of uncertainty and crisis, you need a more personal relationship with your donors.

Let's be more specific. There are three types of tasks you are working on in fundraising, whether you are in crisis or not:

- Recruiting new donors—people who are giving for the first time
- Renewing current donors—keeping the donors you already have
- Developing major donors—upgrading people who have started with smaller gifts

Every strategy that you use should be chosen because it asks people either to give for the first time, renew their gift, or give more than they are currently giving. These are the three functions of fundraising. They are more formally called acquisition, retention, and upgrade. The goals you set in your fundraising plan will include the number of donors you want as well as a dollar amount sought for each of these functions.

Acquiring New Donors

Many organizations are in a crisis right now because they don't have enough donors. Some don't have any donors. These groups' fundraising plans will be built around getting people to give for the first time. If that is your situation, rather than turning automatically to mass direct mail programs, think about a strategy that may be more labor intensive but will yield a much higher percentage of response, such as a house party program or personal letters inviting friends and colleagues to join your organization.

One organization that used to send twenty thousand pieces of direct mail a year and receive an excellent 1.5 percent response, or three hundred new donors, from this program has cut it back to five thousand pieces of mail and replaced mail with other strategies. They are able to focus their mail program on the most likely prospects, boosting their response to 2 percent, or one hundred new donors. A phone canvass of names generated by board members, other donors, and from lapsed-donor lists has gotten a 10 percent response and has brought in one hundred donors from one thousand names. Three long-time volunteers have held house parties and brought in another twenty-five donors each.

For much less money spent, this group has gotten 275 new donors in one year, plus they are getting bigger gifts. Their median gift from direct mail used to be $40, now their median gift from all these strategies is $60. Using personal notes on their renewal letters has also upped their retention rate by almost 8 percent.

Retaining Donors

Organizations that have donors but have not paid much attention to them will need to mount a significant renewal campaign, including more focus on keeping donors and bringing back lapsed donors. Groups that have done a good job of keeping donors but have not spent much time asking those donors to give more will need to focus on major gifts. Most groups will need to do some of each.

Upgrading Donors to Major Gifts

One thing that changes during a recession is whom you will focus your major donor efforts on. In economic boom times, it makes sense to focus your major donor time on people who can give gifts of appreciated assets. But now you need to focus on donors who are giving out of income. For those people, the recession has not taken a heavy toll. For most of them, this year is the same as last year and the year before. They have the same amount of income and a secure job. Anyone in that position, which even today comprises the majority of employed adults, can give this year what they gave last year and the year before. If they are not giving to their capacity, they can be asked for more. You should particularly focus your major donor efforts on people who give between $100 and $1,500. This is about the most neglected group of donors in America. It is easy to understand why.

If someone gives $35 to an organization, they expect a thank-you note, a newsletter, and an invitation to renew their gift at some point. By and large, they get what they expect. If someone gives $5,000 to a group, they get not only a thank-you note but also probably a call from a board member or the executive director. They receive the newsletter as well as occasional other pieces of information. They may get an invitation to a special reception, and they will probably be visited by a staff or board member. They expect that kind of treatment. If they don't want to be dealt with more personally in this way, they will give anonymously.

The person who gives $500, however, when that is a lot of money to them, may also expect a little more specialized treatment but they probably won't get it. The organization will probably send them a nice thank-you note. They may get invited to something special but they will probably not be visited or called personally unless the organization has a very good donor program in place. This group—those who can give $100 to $1,500—if treated a little more personally would likely give more if asked. Few of the people who give $250 a year will have had the experience of being approached more personally. They may be a little cautious at first but most of them will be pleased with the attention, even if they do not increase their giving.

FUNDRAISING AS A TEAM EFFORT

Putting all this in place will require having more than two or three people involved in fundraising. The board of directors needs to play a role and now is a good time to get the board involved. There are many ways for board members to participate in fundraising, from writing thank-you notes and making thank-you calls to writing personal letters asking for upgrades, hosting house parties, and asking for large amounts of money in person. There is no time for the excuse, "I don't like fundraising." What is it that they don't like? Phone calls? Fine, then this board member won't be asked to make calls. Face-to-face asking? Fine, then that board member won't be asked to call on people in person. But the range of tasks is too vast for someone to truly claim, "I cannot do anything with regard to fundraising."

Many organizations have such serious problems involving board members in fundraising that they cannot wait for the board to get its act together before they start raising money. If your organization is in that position, form a team of five or six people, including one or two from the board and the rest committed volunteers, program staff, or community people who believe in your organization. They will take on the fundraising tasks that have been described or alluded to here. They will also take on the task of recruiting more people to the fundraising team.

If you are in a financial crisis, focus on how much money you need for the next quarter or even just for the next month. Break everything down into manageable, time-limited tasks and assign them to a bigger team.

THE DIFFERENCE BETWEEN A GROUP AND A TEAM

Jennifer Henderson (2002), one of the nation's leading organizational development consultants, points out that all organizations start off as a group, but to truly grow and thrive, they eventually must become a team. A group of people gets together and decides what must be done. They each then leave the meeting, do what they said, and report back at the next meeting. Over time, it becomes clear who is reliable and who is not. The group works around the unreliable people by not asking them to do too much. A smaller group of people does most of the work and a larger group pretends to help and perhaps occasionally does.

In a team, there is no room on the field for someone who doesn't want to play. In the sidebar, Henderson identifies fourteen differences between a group and a team and asks organizations to look at the ways they function like a group and the ways they function like a team. This exercise helps groups identify how they need to change to move from group behavior to functioning as a team. From a fundraising viewpoint, the most important elements of being a team are having a goal and a time frame to meet the goal. We cannot postpone the third quarter until Sarah Jones comes back from her trip to do the fundraising that will make that quarter successful. When one person doesn't do their job, the whole team suffers and the job can only get done with the help of the team, even if the team has a star player.

MAKING NEEDED COURSE CORRECTIONS

Organizations that use this time of crisis to really make the course corrections in their fundraising that they need to make and prioritize creating a fundraising team as well as building and maintaining a broad base of individual donors—things we should all have been doing all along—will experience uncertainty as a vital and important part of planning. They will be well prepared for whatever comes down the road because their organizations will have a wide range of sources of money that can be raised with flexible, malleable strategies by a wide range of committed staff and volunteers. Volunteer and staff commitment will be easier to sustain because fundraising is flexible and there are a lot of strategies to choose from. Organizations with a variety of income streams and a well-trained and practiced group of volunteers helping to raise money will be attractive to new volunteers, who will see that they are given the skills they need to do the work.

Groups Versus Teams.

GROUPS	TEAMS
1. The composition of the group changes from meeting to meeting—often without forethought.	1. The composition is planned and is set.
2. Members of groups are encouraged to take on jobs, positions, or tasks even if they are unprepared or not skilled in that area—and everybody knows it!	2. People are recruited, groomed, and trained for specific jobs that match their interests and the needs of the team.
3. People move in and out of jobs based on their inability to say no when asked. Little or no training or support is given by the group to individuals accepting jobs.	3. Each job has a specific set of skills. People with those skills or the ability to acquire them are recruited for the job.
4. Leadership is often one-person deep, with the group highly dependent on a handful of people.	4. Teams have rookies and understudies who learn from those who are accomplished. They are preparing for the day they will lead.
5. When people either do not perform well or fail to perform at all, the group rarely acknowledges the failure.	5. When people do not perform well, the team suffers. The team has ways of assisting the person or has systems for building the person's skills or moving him or her to another position.
6. Groups often resist planning and use planning as corrective rather than proactive or preventive strategies. Planning is mostly done by a few people.	6. The planning by teams is called practice, run-throughs, or rehearsals. No matter how talented any individual team member, everyone plans.
7. Groups rarely create routine operations.	7. Teams have rituals, routines, and ceremonies that everyone learns and shares.
8. Groups usually do not celebrate or debrief victories or defeats.	8. Teams regularly review performance. Teams often prepare for the next piece of work based on the evaluation of the last piece of work.
9. Groups rarely assess their progress in achieving their stated goals or objectives in order to chart and measure their work.	9. Teams know at most times how they are doing—if they are winning, scoring, or moving toward their stated goals.
10. Groups may or may not celebrate the accomplishments of past leadership.	10. Teams often establish "Halls of Fame," retiring an honored jersey. Those who have performed well are held in high esteem.

Groups Versus Teams. *(Continued)*

11. Members of groups are often hard to identify. There is rarely anything linking them to the group.	11. Members of teams are easily recognizable. There are usually colors, logos, T-shirts, and most important, common slang, songs, language, and history to link them to each other and the team.
12. Groups are often inconsistent in what time things start and end—especially meetings!	12. Time is important to teams. Most events have specific starting and ending times. Teams are often judged by what they can accomplish within a certain time frame.
13. Groups sometimes operate without thinking about their constituency.	13. Teams understand how important it is to consider the fans, the audience, everyone affected by the game. Teams know and respect the game's many stakeholders.
14. Groups sometimes fail to develop a sense of team spirit. They assume everyone understands and works together.	14. Teams build team spirit into their plans and make sure to affirm and celebrate the work they accomplish together.

Source: Henderson, 2002, p. 10.

Finally, flexible organizations with experience in managing a diversity of funding sources and with a diverse team of fundraisers will do much better at attracting the broad array of new donors who are on the horizon. These demographics will vary from place to place, but they will include people between the ages of eighteen and twenty-five—people giving to your organization and indeed to any organization for the first time—along with new immigrants, who have often been left out of traditional fundraising. Immigrants and people of color will form the majority of the United States population by 2050 and even now are the majority of the population of many states, including California, Colorado, New Mexico, and New York. Fundraising approaches are already changing as these diverse populations bring their own giving traditions and create new ones. Flexible organizations need to be ahead of this curve.

Creating a flexible fundraising program is not just a way to get through a crisis—it is the foundation for growing and thriving on uncertainty.

Here are two examples of organizations that used the tools described in the last three chapters to get out of a crisis and, month by month, to stay out of one.

Clearview Community Center

A well-loved and well-used community center in a town of fifty thousand people is accused by a columnist of the local newspaper of sheltering terrorists because it allows a Palestinian organization to hold monthly meetings there. The Palestinian organization raises money for medical supplies to be sent to the occupied territories in Israel and helps new immigrants from the Middle East find housing and jobs in the Clearview community. Suddenly the community center is in the middle of a firestorm of controversy. Letters supporting or condemning the center fill up the "Letters to the Editor" columns of the local paper. A family foundation decides not to renew a large grant to the community center on the basis that it has become "political." The local newspaper columnist next insinuates that people may be accused of collaborating with terrorists if they use the center for events. Within a month, some organizations cancel their events and the center's income shrinks.

A few board members come together to discuss the situation and, finding themselves divided over what to do, do nothing. Some want to ask the Palestinian group to leave, others believe that they should ask for an apology and a retraction from the newspaper, and others feel that they should just let the situation blow over. Their inaction appears to the outside world as ineptness.

The community center's events coordinator, who is also the only staff person, puts together a Crisis Task Force made up of people who use the center regularly. They develop a message: the center is important to the whole community, which means everyone. They write a Letter to the Editor describing the importance of the center to the town and have it signed by dozens of groups that have used the center over the years. The letter makes clear that it is not from the center's board, but that a number of organizations are concerned with keeping the center open to all. They note that a gay Republican organization has met there, as well as a group of women seeking ordination in the Catholic church.

The task force then organizes a door-to-door canvass to go twenty blocks in each direction from the center to ask for money as well as explain the mission of the center. Fifty people set out in pairs on a Saturday afternoon. They have so many conversations with neighbors that they are not able to cover their whole territory. They are able, however, to quell a lot of anxiety and they find that the center has a lot of support. People give money who went to their first high school dance at the center, who support the film festival at the center every fall, who believe that the columnist for the paper is a bigot. The name of each donor is written down, even if the donation is in cash, unless the donor asks for anonymity. The following day, thank-you notes are sent to every donor signed by two people—the chair of the Palestinian organization and the center's events coordinator, who is well known in the community. This is high-touch fundraising.

The community center's Web site is also used to gather support, offering readers the opportunity to send an e-mail to the editor of the paper expressing their opinion and to donate on-line. These strategies not only raise money, they also mobilize people to write to the newspaper; eventually the columnist retracts his accusation. Several of the organizations that canceled events reconsider and reschedule.

The group must still replace the grant they lost, but they have time. Their real problem now becomes obvious—a lackluster, uncommitted board. The task force proposes that the most inactive board members resign and replace themselves with the task force members. Seeing an easy way out, most board members agree to the plan.

The community center can now put together a community board, unite behind a mission, and continue its excellent work. Ironically, this crisis has worked well for them.

Youth Organizing Now (YO!NOW)

This three-year-old youth-serving organization has financed itself entirely with two foundation grants and the money that their three young founders were awarded from various fellowships and programs for new and emerging leaders. The founders, who are also the staff, used their awards to cover their salaries; the foundation grants have paid for rent, phones, computers, and the like. The founders are also three of the five board members, along with two other friends, because they don't really believe in the corporate structure of a nonprofit.

The organization works with high school and college students on a variety of issues determined by the young people themselves. They have addressed mandatory testing in the schools, police brutality, sexual harassment, and issues of globalization. The program focuses on the process of organizing—creating a series of demands, doing enough research so they can't be discredited, and getting media attention. Learning organizing tactics is more important to this group than focusing on any particular issue, although it makes the organization a little hard to explain to funders and donors.

The group has no individual donor program and does not include fundraising in their organizing curriculum. The group's fellowships and awards are running out and their foundation grants are ending. One foundation has changed direction and is no longer focused on youth; the other is cutting back because of a precipitous drop in assets. YO!NOW's staff had counted on getting two other grants that would carry them through the next year, but both of those have been turned down. Suddenly, they have two months' worth of money left and no new money coming in. They feel they can't raise enough money from their youth members to stay open and they don't want to seek major gifts from "rich people" (not that they know any).

They form a Crisis Task Force with themselves, one high school student, two college students, and a young professor from the university. Recommitting to mission, they see that their goal of empowering young people lacks an important component: financial empowerment. On reflection, they realize that fundraising needs to be part of their organizing curriculum. They also like the idea of creating some earned income. One staff person notes that they are asked several times a week for written versions of their organizing curriculum, or to help work with high school students or integrate young people into programs in a meaningful way. What if they decided to sell the information they have developed? What if they decided to charge for their consultations, which are now free and very casual, but also time-consuming? They ask a consultant to join their task force to help them price their services, and the students seek help from other faculty in pricing the written materials. When they explain why they are developing this earned-income stream, people—including faculty, staff of other nonprofits, and some trainers and consultants—offer them donations. YO!NOW realizes that their work is impressive and that people are happy to help them.

In the short term, YO!NOW is able to generate money from consulting work and teaching workshops on various aspects of dealing with youth. A marketing student takes on development and marketing of their materials as his class assignment. The materials are posted on their Web site, where they can be downloaded for a fee. This income will not be enough to support the organization in the long term, but it will be a steady and reliable source.

Over the longer term, though, this organization has a tough road ahead. They have no infrastructure for keeping track of donations, no system for thanking people, no newsletter or other way of keeping in touch with donors, and no plan for increasing their number of donors. Though they make a commitment to integrate fundraising into their curriculum, they don't really know how to do so. However, if they can keep themselves open, one month at a time, they are perfectly capable of learning all they need to know.

CHAPTER 6

Designing Your Short-Term Strategy

B y now, you are probably thinking, "All of this is fine, but what are we supposed to do *right now?*" In this chapter, you will learn how to raise money immediately so that you can buy your organization some time to do the retooling and rethinking you may need to do.

To raise money in a hurry, you need a strategy that does not require much front money. As you can imagine, any strategy like that will involve a great deal of personal solicitation. This requirement is usually the first stumbling block. As discussed in Chapter Two, part of the background of the current crisis in the nonprofit sector is the ongoing inability or reluctance of otherwise very dedicated volunteers to ask for money. There have been thousands of workshops, hundreds of articles, dozens of books, and even a few videos devoted to this theme. I should know, having contributed quantities of material in all these forms. I will not repeat what can easily be found elsewhere (see Resources), except to say that most people remain uptight and hesitant about asking for money until they internalize five simple principles:

1. *Most people, when offered the opportunity to give money to your group, will say no.* They may say no directly: "No, I can't help you." They may say no by never responding to your letters or calls. They may say no by saying, "I'll think about it" and never getting back to you. Or even, sadly, they may

say no by saying yes and then never paying their pledge. Nonetheless, enough people will say yes to make it worth continuing to ask. But you must ask far more people than the number of gifts you need. In fact, even when asking friends who you know give away money and who you know care about the cause you represent, you still need to ask four friends for every one gift you will receive. Two of your four friends will give nothing, the third person will give you less than you asked for, and the fourth one may give you the amount you asked for. (I give more detailed information about response rates in Chapter Nine.)

2. *It has to be OK with you for people to say no.* Not only does no need to be OK with you, you should think of a *no* as a good thing—as putting you one step closer to a *yes.* When you go for a whole week without getting a *no,* it is because you have not asked enough people. Your job is to ask, to offer other people the opportunity to give to your group. The people you ask must be people who give away money, as do seven out of ten adults. They are going to give the money somewhere and your job is to get on their menu. The person being asked also has a job—their job is to take you up on your offer or to turn you down. What they do will depend on their mood, their financial circumstance, their other commitments, their confidence in the future or lack of it—many variables that you can't do anything about and that are not about you.

3. *What you believe in has to be bigger than what you are afraid of.* If you don't like asking for money, or you would rather not do it, or you wish someone else would do it for you, that is normal. That is how most people feel. Money is a loaded subject, full of meanings that are way beyond the item itself. You can spend a lot of time analyzing what you don't like about asking for money and that will be time well spent. But if you don't have the time to do such an analysis, or you have spent the time and you still don't feel good about asking for money, I suggest you think about what is going to happen if you don't ask anyone for money. What will happen to your organization? Does it matter if your organization goes out of business? If it matters to you, then put the desire to keep your organization afloat first, ahead of your anxiety about asking. There is an old fundraising saying, "If

you are afraid to ask for money, kick yourself out of the way and let the cause talk."

4. *You will need to ask some people, but you don't have to ask everyone.* Many people never get out of the starting gate because they think they have to ask everyone they know. They then imagine how awful it would be to ask their neighbor or their ex-husband or their Aunt Mildred. Don't ask people whom you have difficult relationships with or who don't believe in your cause. Start with someone very easy: yourself. Make your own gift first. Make sure your gift is significant for you—that you feel it and it feels good. Then go to friends and family members whom you like and who like you and agree with the cause you represent. If you really don't like to ask people you know, then ask people you don't know—donors to the organization whom you have not met or donors to another organization similar to yours. But make sure you are asking people who both give away money and believe in your cause or a cause similar to yours.

5. *Put yourself in the donor's shoes.* You may not like asking but that doesn't mean the donor doesn't want to be asked. Most people like to be seen as helpful and generous. They like to be included. Sometimes organizations go out of business and people around the organization will say, "I never knew they were in trouble. Why didn't they ask for help?" Once, a close friend of the board chair of a failing group told me, "I would help if he would ask, but I get the feeling that he doesn't want my help. Maybe what I have to give isn't good enough." There are far more hurt feelings from not being included and not being asked than there ever will be from being asked.

Saturate your mind with these five points. Tape them above your desk, on your bathroom mirror, and write them in your calendar or Palm Pilot. Read them when you wake up and when you go to sleep. Start every meeting by reminding each person of these five points. Within a week, you will be 50 percent more comfortable with asking for money; in two weeks, you will be another 50 percent more comfortable. The more you ask, the more comfortable you will get. Also, not surprisingly, the more you ask, the more money you will get.

WHERE TO START

The Crisis Task Force starts by determining the amount of money the organization needs for *the next three months.* Include any debt that may have accumulated, but use common sense in choosing a number. If you are in profound debt, you may have to postpone paying back the debt. At this point, do not plan to cut anything. (If, however, maintaining the status quo leaves you with too big a number to raise, you may have to cut a program to give yourself a reasonable fundraising challenge.) Now create a very simple gift-range chart, one with at most four layers:

One gift = 25 percent of the goal.

Two gifts = 25 percent of the goal.

Four gifts = 25 percent of the goal.

Eight gifts = 25 percent of the goal.

Fifteen gifts = 100 percent of the goal.

Fifteen gifts × four prospects per gift = sixty people who need to be asked.

Of the sixty people who need to be asked, half, or thirty, will give nothing; the other thirty will give something. Fifteen of the thirty who say yes will give less than they are asked for. The remaining fifteen will give the amount requested. If these are all in the lower ranges of the chart, the additional fifteen less-than-asked-for gifts will help meet the fundraising goal.

FINDING THE "INNER CIRCLE" OF PROSPECTS

Now that you know how much you need and from how many people, you can focus on who those people are.

A number of years ago, a friend's daughter got into serious trouble with drugs. She needed to go to a residential rehabilitation program, but she did not have health insurance and her mother did not have the $10,000 the program cost. My friend and I sat down with two other close friends and made a list of people who cared about this young woman. We looked for twenty people who could give between $250 and $1,000 each. My friend's instinct was to say that she didn't know anyone who could give much more than $100. When the three of us each pledged $500, she saw she was wrong and admitted that it was hard for her to talk about her daughter's addiction. "That's why we are helping you and why we are going to people like ourselves," we said. We raised the $10,000 in two days.

That was a lesson to me about identifying your inner circle of people. Unless your organization is very isolated, it has such a circle. Whether that circle has enough money to bail you out is another question. But you are only looking for enough money to get you through the next three months while you figure out what you are going to do. As the example of YO!NOW in the previous chapter showed, sometimes you are operating month-to-month.

Make a list of people who you think really care about your organization. They may be passionate about the mission—former board members, former staff people, volunteers, former volunteers. They may have been helped by your organization and feel grateful. They may be vendors with whom you do a lot of business and who would not like to lose the income.

Next add people who might be willing to help you just this once—parents and grandparents, sisters and brothers, best friends of staff, board, and volunteers. In this instance, they don't need to believe 100 percent in the cause because there is no expectation that they will be continuing to give after helping out this one time. (Of course, each donor should be offered the opportunity to become a regular donor, but make sure you respect their wishes if giving only once is what they want.) Don't forget to look through your current donor list. There are bound to be people in this group who can make gifts of the size you need *in addition* to what they are giving now, especially if they believe that you will not get into this situation again. Remember, capacity to give is only one variable. How the prospects feel about the crisis and how it is being handled is the key variable. Whether they feel confident that you won't be coming to them every few months for a bail-out gift is a related element. Remember to keep on repeating the message here, and don't emphasize the crisis—emphasize the work you will be able to do with the money.

Of course, a lot depends on how much money you need right away. If your goal is more than $100,000, and you don't have people who can help you with gifts of $25,000, $10,000, and $5,000, you may have to set up a line of credit or think about raising only enough money for one month while you put longer-range strategies in place. If your goal is $10,000, you may decide to go with fewer gifts.

To decide which amount on your gift-range chart to ask someone for, look for the following qualities.

If the person is already a donor, look at the following:

A. *They have given your organization money for three or more years.* Donors with three or more years of giving history can be asked to double their gift. Depending on what you know about them, this request might be presented as a one-time appeal to get through this immediate crisis or as a request for an annual upgrade as part of your ongoing need to raise money in a different way than you have before.

B. *The donor is already giving what is a large gift for them.* You know this is a large gift because they have said so. They have been asked personally. However, a donor who is always able to make a large gift in one payment can usually give at least one more time during the year when there is a special circumstance. They can't give that much to every group and they may not wish to give that much a second time every year, but they have the capacity to give a second gift of the same size.

C. *The donor gives to "special appeals."* Donors who always buy a table at an event, or give an extra gift at year end, or respond to newsletter requests, can be asked to give an additional gift. This may or may not be the same size as their regular gift.

Donors in group A need to be asked personally, first with a personal letter followed by a phone call and possibly a meeting.

Approach donors in group B with a special letter asking for an extra gift of the same size as their regular gift. Personalize the letter by addressing it to them personally and beginning it with "Dear Terry" or "Dear Ms. Smith and Mr. Brown." That is the extent of the personalization, as the same letter is going to out to everyone in that category and the letters will not carry a personal note. Ideally, follow up by phone. The letter talks about the crisis and its positive resolution (see the following section) and comes with a return envelope.

Donors in group C will get a special appeal asking for more money; this is similar to appeals you might be sending anyway.

Some donors will fall into more than one category. When that is the case, give them more personal treatment.

If the person has not given before, look at the following:

If the prospect is not currently a donor to your organization, you will need to make your best guess about the amount to ask for. You may wish to show them your gift-range chart and ask if they can see themselves in any of those categories. If you know what they give to other organizations, that will give you a sense of what to ask for. You can always phrase your request as, "I am not sure how much to ask you for. We need gifts of every amount. Every gift will be well spent and most appreciated. Could you consider a gift in the _____ range?" This gives the prospect plenty of wiggle room but also mitigates against asking for a gift that is too small.

THE LETTER

In previous chapters, we have talked about what you are going to say about the crisis. Now we need to talk about what you are going to *write* about the crisis to people outside of the immediate "family."

First, remember that writing is permanent. You need to examine what you write to make sure it is true and that it can't be subject to misinterpretation. What you write may eventually be read by anyone, so make sure that it will withstand being read by someone who is not sympathetic to your situation. Be especially careful with e-mail, which often gets forwarded, taking on a life of its own. People often dash off an e-mail in the same way they would make a passing comment. A comment may be forgotten; even if repeated, it gradually loses its punch. But an e-mail comment has the same weight always.

Whatever you write about the crisis gives the crisis some permanence. What you don't want to do is give the crisis priority over your work. Donors should support you because your work is very important and not because you are going to have to shut your doors if you don't get any money. Your need for money is boring. Some 1.5 million organizations could make the same claim, as could billions of people. The fact that you need money only reminds others that they need money too. What you need the money *for* is primary. That you need it in a hurry may be part of the pitch, but the need alone is not going to raise money.

Let's look at two possible letters to donors who have given an organization $500 or more for three or more years. They are going to be asked to consider doubling their gift. The organization is a ten-year-old nonsectarian retreat center. After a grease fire burned a guest, the center's industrial kitchen was condemned by the county as unsafe because the organization did not have proper sprinklers and fire extinguishers in place. A dot-com millionaire had pledged the entire $150,000 needed for the renovation and had paid $25,000. Before he could pay more, his company went bankrupt, his stock became worthless, and now he cannot complete the pledge. Without the kitchen, the organization cannot accommodate overnight retreats and is losing a lot of business. The publicity surrounding the grease fire has died down, but it was not positive.

From the Chair of the Board
Dear Jane Donor,

This year marks the third year you have supported Deep Valley Renewal Center, and I thank you very much for your gifts. Your support has allowed us to increase the number of classes we offer, make ourselves available to organizations that cannot pay market rates for conference space, and be a welcoming space for writers, people wanting time for a retreat, travelers, and others.

We pride ourselves on being a safe space—we welcome men and women of all ages, races, and sexual orientation. The campus's "universal design" makes it fully wheelchair accessible. To truly be a Renewal Center, it must feel warm and welcoming. So, you can imagine our deep chagrin when our kitchen proved to be anything but safe. As you may know from the news coverage, an unsafe stove set off a grease fire that burned much longer than it should have because we didn't have proper fire retardants in place. Worst of all, a guest was hurt. (We are thankful to say he is now fully recovered.)

These unsafe conditions are not what we stand for or believe in, and it is our highest priority to fix the kitchen and get the Renewal Center back up to full capacity.

I am hopeful that you will join me to help fund this capital improvement campaign. Would you consider doubling your gift this year to $1,000?

I have doubled my own pledge, and I can tell you it feels good and it makes it easier for me to ask others to consider doing the same. I realize this is a big commitment. I will call you in a few days to discuss it further.

Whatever you are able to do to help restore the center's kitchen facilities, know how grateful we are for what you have already done. We look forward to welcoming you back to Deep Valley Renewal Center in the very near future.

Sincerely,

Betty Lou Boardchair

From the Executive Director

Dear Jane Donor,

I write with an urgent request. As you probably read in the paper, our kitchen has been condemned by the county. It had been in disrepair for some time, and recently a fire destroyed it. To rebuild it as a hospitable and fully usable space will cost $150,000. A generous donor has given the first $25,000 and now we are turning to donors like you for the rest.

I am hoping you can help with an extra $500 or $1,000 for this unexpected capital expense. We know that if enough donors are willing to make an extra gift beyond their annual donation, we can raise the remaining $125,000 that we need.

I or someone from the board will call you in the next ten days to answer any questions you have and to thank you personally for all your support over the past three years. I enclose a return envelope for your convenience.

Thank you for whatever you can do,

Harried Executive Director

Depending on Jane Donor's personality, either letter will work. The first one emphasizes the overall commitment of the Renewal Center and the breach in commitment the fire caused. The second letter gets to the point more quickly and focuses more on the immediate need. The letters can be this different because they are from different people. The board chair writes as a peer, one donor to another. The executive director writes as a person absorbed in the day-to-day running of the center. In both these letters, we have an example of the importance of message—the message in this case is that the kitchen fire is something the group is determined will never happen again because of the organization's larger commitment to being a welcoming and safe space. Nothing else needs to be said.

FOLLOW-UP

Of course, nothing will come of either letter without follow-up—most often by telephone, but sometimes in a visit. Some or all of the members of the Crisis Task Force will be involved in following up on the letters sent (see the following discussion).

You should space your letters so that you do not have to follow up with more than four or five people in any given week. Wait until one or two days after you think the person would have received the letter, then call.

Before the call, think through what you are going to say. What will you say if you get voice mail, which is the most likely outcome of your call? What if you get a personal assistant or someone else in the prospect's family? What if you get the prospect?

Fundraising in Times of Crisis

Your message should be brief. If you reach the prospect, your first message should be one of respect for that person. Say your name followed by, "Do you have a minute to talk?" If the answer is yes, ask if they got the letter. If yes, build off what they seem to know, or if no, summarize the letter succinctly. In either case, briefly say what you want: "I want to thank you for what you have done for Good Group in the past and ask you to consider doing more in the future." Always say the whole name of your organization, not its initials or acronym. Be specific about what you want the donor to consider: doubling their gift, making a one-time-only gift, considering a meeting, attending an event. Don't use any more words than are necessary to convey that you are thankful for what they have done, appreciate their time on the phone right now, and want them to consider doing something more. Pause to let the prospect talk. Don't say more than two or three sentences without pausing.

Take your cues about what to say from the prospect. For example, if the prospect says "I don't know if I can do any more," you say "Please feel free to think about it. You don't have to give an answer right now. Is there anything I can tell you now that will help in your thinking?" Set a time to reconnect: "Should I call you back in a few days?" or "How shall we be in touch?" Many people prefer e-mail as a way to stay in touch and you may want to offer that option.

If the prospect raises issues about the crisis itself, listen and don't get defensive. Remember, you have had whole meetings to process your feelings and figure out what happened. This person has not had that advantage and now they are going to use you. Tell the truth, but stick to the message. If you have correctly identified this prospect as one of the "inner circle," he or she will ultimately want what is best for the organization. The degree to which they are angry or disappointed or judgmental needs to be seen as reflecting how much they care.

Before making any phone calls, members of the committee making calls should practice with each other so that they have answers ready that they feel good about. As the team makes follow-up calls, they should note what people say and bring that back to the group. You will be surprised at how many people are not focused on the crisis and, unless it has gotten a lot of publicity, may not have heard about it at all. They may be curious or even nosy, but they have a lot going on in their own life and the crisis that is absorbing so much of your time is a temporary distraction for most of them.

TIMING AND ASSIGNMENTS

The letters, the follow-up calls, and the visits, if any, should be done in a two- to four-week period. Remember, you won't need to visit most prospects. Only those prospects in Group A discussed earlier in the chapter should receive an invitation to be visited. Of that group, many will decide what they want to do as a result of the phone conversation. If your organization works nationally or serves a large region, don't offer to visit people unless their gift is very large. You can say in your phone call, "I hope we will get a chance to meet some time, but because of the immediacy of this crisis and the distance involved, we are conducting this campaign largely by phone."

There are two ways to think about who does what. Assuming you have at least six people on your team and you are contacting the sixty prospects needed to reach the gift-range goal described previously, one division of labor is for six people to contact five prospects a week for two weeks. This is the most even division of labor.

Another way to proceed is for two people to contact those donors who should receive offers of visits, because the process of setting up and then going on a visit takes so much more time than a phone call. Members of the team who go on visits will have fewer prospects than team members whose follow-up consists only of calling.

Send the letter out to the first five prospects, wait three days, and begin calling. Send a letter to the next five prospects sometime in the middle of the first week and call them the second week. You may have to call more than once, but don't leave more than three messages. The idea of this campaign is to raise the money quickly from people who don't need a whole lot of hand-holding. These people are buying you time to set up a proper fundraising program and to deal with other elements of the crisis in the next three months.

LEARNING TO BE A GRACIOUS RECEIVER

Many times, organizations are amazed and gratified at what their donors and prospects are willing to do for them. In addition to the money, the morale boost from support in a crisis helps rally everyone and keeps the Crisis Task Force, staff, and board members energized for the hard work required to get out of this crisis and stay out of future ones.

Many people are raised, as I was, to be self-reliant by learning how to solve their own problems and be of service to others. However, the shadow side of self-reliance is learning that being part of a community means not only helping others but allowing oneself to ask for help and be helped. For me, part of learning to ask for money involved also learning to be a gracious receiver. Those of us who give time, money, and our talent often don't like to ask for things, especially money. A crisis helps us learn how to be gracious receivers. We can't get through a crisis without help, nor should we even try. Because an organization needs to reflect its community, our job is to allow the community to be involved. A crisis provides an opportunity to engage the community further and build such involvement into the way we work now and in the future.

CHAPTER 7

Fundraising Strategies for the Next Six to Twelve Months

While you are raising enough money to get you through the most immediate crisis, as soon as you can you must begin planning strategies to get you through the next six months to one year. Otherwise, you are simply a group in remission from a terminal condition rather than a group on the mend. For most organizations, this next period is the hardest. A colleague's experience after an accident provides a good example of the difficulties of times of healing:

> I was in a car accident and was very banged up, with broken ribs and a broken leg. Friends were great. They came to the hospital in droves. One brought me home to a house full of people and for about ten days friends came with food and kept me company. Someone cleaned my house and someone else did my laundry. But after about two weeks, everyone was back in their own lives. I was much better and could hobble around but I still needed help. The crisis was over, but I wasn't recovered. At that point, my neighbor started helping me. He did my dishes and helped me get dressed. He took me to physical therapy.
>
> I realized that I am the kind of friend who responds immediately and then goes back to my life. I'm the kind you need in an

emergency. My neighbor did not visit me in the hospital and did not come over very much at first. He is the kind of friend who is not as helpful in an emergency and will not spend huge chunks of time with you, but is willing to do things you need help with every day over many days. That's the kind you need when you are healing but not healed.

Organizations go through the same phases as my colleague did after his accident. After you get through the immediate crisis, you need friends—donors and volunteers—of the longer-term, lower-key variety. There is, of course, some overlap between one group of helpers and another, and if you haven't burned out your volunteers completely, many of them will convert to the long-term types you need.

THE END OF THE CRISIS TASK FORCE

After three or four months, your crisis task force should dissolve. They have done their job, and if they have been able to do it right, you are on a different path than the one that led you into the crisis. Most of these people will, we hope, still be available for various fundraising tasks from time to time. Their work should also have surfaced some people who want to help you for the longer term. These may be board members who are reinvigorated and have a better understanding of their role, donors who have been brought closer to the work of the group and want to keep helping, or staff members who are not in the development department but who understand the need for integrating fundraising into their work as much as possible.

SCALED-BACK FUNDRAISING

The strategies you will pursue to get you through the next year are simply miniversions of the traditional fundraising strategies that you will use for the long term. However, there are several differences in scale between how you raise money for the next twelve months and what you will be doing when you are fully back on your feet. For example, you will do small mail

Fundraising in Times of Crisis

appeals because you don't have a lot of front money and because you are still figuring out a profile of your donors; you will do small-scale fundraising events to keep cash flowing in. You will continue personal solicitation for larger gifts, and you may even pursue some foundation funding, although if that is what got you into this mess in the first place, you will want to be cautious about how much time you put into that strategy.

EVALUATING FUNDRAISING ACTIVITIES

Get in the habit of evaluating your fundraising. In order to really know what works for your organization and why, you need to take the time to debrief every strategy that you pursue. Write up a report about whatever strategies you use and include the following information:

Strategy
- Purpose of strategy besides raising money (acquire new donors, renew donors, approach major donors, raise money from places or people who wouldn't give otherwise)
- Volunteer time required and number of volunteers required
- Staff time required
- Budget—itemized expenses and income
- Time line
- Evaluation of strategy

   Did it meet its goals?

   What would we do exactly the same next time?

   How can we do this event with less time?

   What would we do differently next time?

By systematically evaluating everything you do, even if you only make brief comments for each of the questions, you will learn what works for your organization and how it can work better. You will still be working harder on your fundraising now than you will need to later, but you should be putting in fewer hours than when the crisis struck.

STRATEGIES

Choosing fundraising strategies can be confusing. In the rest of this chapter, I outline several strategies that are appropriate for raising money during the six to twelve months after the crisis has been identified. This is when the organization is beginning to heal and make the permanent changes needed in its fundraising programs.

Every fundraising strategy has a series of tasks to accomplish them successfully. Many how-to books and Web sites provide that detailed information (see Resources for some suggestions), so I haven't supplied all the details you need. However, I have given enough information here for you to choose some you will want to pursue further. Obviously, you won't choose all of the following, and you may well choose a number of other fundraising activities that I haven't listed. But I hope you will put your plan together using some of the criteria I have used in selecting and describing these strategies.

Saturday Yard, Tag, or Garage Sale

Income. Expect to earn between $1,000 and $5,000.

Workers Needed Prior to the Sale. You'll need two to find a space to have the sale, store stuff, and advertise the sale.

Workers Needed the Day Before and the Morning of the Sale. You'll need four to price everything and set up on the morning of the sale. (These can include the previous two or it can be four new people.)

Workers Needed the Day of the Sale Itself. You'll need two or three for every two hours the sale is on. One stands by the money and one circulates, bargaining with people. (You can add an extra income stream by selling baked goods, but this requires more workers.)

Keep in Mind. Location is key. The ideal space is a parking lot for a business that is only open during the week, such as a doctor's or dentist's office, a bank, or an empty storefront if you think the weather could be bad. Make sure it is on a busy street so that many people will see your sale.

Upside of This Strategy. Many people know how to do these types of sales and it is not hard to get stuff donated. You can start by sending an e-mail to everyone you know in the immediate area asking them to donate all their used but usable stuff. Price the stuff, set up the sale, and collect the money. This is a great training opportunity for new volunteers or people who don't like fundraising. Some people love working at these sales, and they are very good at spotting donated items that can be sold for more money. You don't have to explain your crisis or even anything about your group to your buyers, as most people come to the sale just to get bargains.

You can do a good job with this strategy in one month. If you have two or three months, you can advertise more, or decide to sell some of the nicer items on an on-line auction site, or hold the sale over two days.

Downside of This Strategy. Storage before the sale and weather the day of the sale can be real problems. You can get a lot of junk donated and then have to spend precious time disposing of it. The sale does not recruit new donors likely to be loyal.

Phone-a-thon to Current Donors

Income. This varies with number of people in this category. Generally, you will have a positive response to about 10 percent of calls made to current donors. Add-ons: People who have ever given money but aren't current donors and people you would like to invite to become donors. The response from these lists will be about 5 percent of calls made. (Make sure you haven't already approached these people as part of your immediate fundraising plan.)

Workers Needed Prior to the Phone-a-thon. You'll need two or three. They will compile lists, find phone numbers, write up scripts and answers to frequently asked questions.

Workers Needed During the Phone-a-thon. Calculate by using the formula of one worker for every fifty to seventy-five names for each three-hour shift. Volunteers with a lot of calling experience will move through their names faster than new people, who will need to debrief after each call or get a glass of water every time they encounter a rude response. Workers should take a five-minute break every hour and a ten-minute break in the middle of the phone-a-thon.

For Workers Right Before the Phone-a-thon. Provide a training and practice session ahead of the actual calling and make the calling as much fun as possible. Give each person a little bell or clicker to use when they have received a pledge; provide little prizes for the person who gets through the most names, the person who gets the biggest pledge of the evening, or the person who encounters the most rude response. Give everyone who helps a coupon for a free pizza or movie—this is an inexpensive way to reward volunteers.

Workers Needed After the Phone-a-thon. You'll need one or two to send thank-you notes, process credit card numbers, and clean up the database as needed.

Keep in Mind. Some people really dislike being phoned; others use the phone to express their frustration with the rest of their sad life. Callers need to be ready to encounter great rudeness. They should be taught to say, "Would you like me to make sure you are on our no-call list?" This question usually mollifies people and allows the conversation to end civilly.

Upside of This Strategy. This is an easy strategy to complete in two weeks and attracts volunteers who want to help you and are willing to put in a lot of time for a very short period. Some people enjoy working a phone-a-thon and are able to make it a game for themselves and their fellow phoners.

Phone-a-thons are a good way to train people to ask for money because it is somewhat anonymous—even though the volunteer says her name, the caller rarely remembers it—yet it requires talking to a live person.

Phone-a-thons are also an efficient way to clean up your database. You may find out whether people have moved, divorced, or died. By capturing that information you can update your records.

Downside of This Strategy. This strategy can be discouraging to callers if the lists you are using are old and ill-kept. Donors may be rude and sometimes you can have a high rate of bad pledges.

Mini-Major Donor Campaign

Income. This varies widely and depends on how many prospects you have not already contacted as part of the immediate response to your crisis. A small organization should be able to raise $2,500 in one month with this strategy. Subtract $1,000 if you are in a poor and rural community. Add $2,500 if you have a major donor program in place now and you have not already asked your major donors for an extra gift.

You are looking for one gift of $500, four gifts of $250 each, and five gifts of $100 each. These gift amounts are within reach of many working people. You will need about thirty prospects to ask: about fifteen will say no and some will give less than you ask for. However, if a person says no to $250, they may give $100, so you should have ten gifts when you are done. If you cannot find any $500 donors, you will have to raise the number of $250 or $100 donors you need.

Workers Needed. See Chapter Six for details on this strategy.

Upside of This Strategy. This is an easy moneymaker and gives you a chance to find out what donors are thinking and saying about your group. A strategy like this allows you to refine your message.

Downside of This Strategy. You may have used up most of your high-dollar prospects already. Finding volunteers for this one may be difficult, as your best volunteers are probably taking a break from their work on the Crisis Task Force.

Mail Appeal to Current Donors

Income. This varies widely with size of donor base; it should yield a 10 percent response with the same median gift as you get on your annual appeals. You can do this as an add-on: use a similar letter to attract new donors. Count on a 1 percent or 2 percent response from lists of potential donors. This effort will not bring in very much money, but will help you expand your donor base.

Send a mail appeal to all your donors at the $1 to $99 level describing the work you will be doing in the next quarter and asking for an extra gift to support that work. Be specific: "We have fifteen more clients every day than we did before the recession. It costs us $35 an hour to work with each one. They pay what they can, but few can pay more than $5 or $10, as they are either out of work or in minimum-wage jobs. Can you help with an extra gift for these extra clients? A gift of $25 makes up the difference between what we spend and what one client pays. Each gift really helps." Your reply device might have these choices:

- $25 (one client).
- $100 (four clients).
- $375 (one day's worth of new clients).
- $____ whatever you want to give. Every gift is put right to work and is very appreciated.

Workers Needed Prior to the Mailing. You'll need two to compile lists, create letter, and get everything printed.

Workers Needed During the Mailing Party. You'll need three to four to fold, stuff, and seal letters, affix labels, or write addresses and put in the mail.

Upside of This Strategy. This is an easy strategy for shy board members or volunteers, as it does not require any personal solicitation. It is a great way to appeal to people whom you are not that close to but who you think would be interested in your cause.

Downside of This Strategy. It can be a lot of work for not much response. If lists have not been well kept, there can be a high rate of undeliverable letters.

All-Volunteer Door-to-Door Canvass for One Saturday

Income. Generally, you can expect 12 percent of households in the catchment area to contribute something. Each volunteer should be able to raise at least $150 for each three-hour time period. Twenty volunteers (ten in the morning and ten in the afternoon) will raise at least $3,000.

Workers Needed Prior to Canvass. You'll need two or three to map out an area, create a script, and recruit volunteers.

Workers Needed the Day of Canvass. This varies in number, type, and logistics. Include a coordinator to keep track of where everyone is and to take care of money raised as volunteers end their shifts. As many people as possible are needed to walk the route. You will need to decide if you want the canvassers to go in pairs or by themselves. If they go alone, two people should be in the same block or able to check in with each other easily every few households.

Keep in Mind. Make sure you research and obey any city laws concerning getting a permit to canvass.

If you are able to have a public service announcement on the radio with a message such as, "Look for a volunteer from the Rape Crisis Center this Saturday—please be as generous as you can," some people will be expecting you. If in addition you can say, "If you are not home, please go to our Web site and give on-line," you can pick up some extra money that way. Many groups will have a canvasser leave a door-hanger with that message if no one is home.

Some organizations have been able to build a volunteer canvass into a large special event that uses upwards of two hundred people on one Saturday afternoon and raises $30,000 or more. Obviously, something of that scale takes longer than the time allotted here, but if a small-scale volunteer canvass works for your organization, you may want to explore building it into an annual event.

Upside of This Strategy. Although labor-intensive, this strategy can raise a lot of money with little front money required. It is also one of the best ways to get a message out to a specific geographic community and should especially be considered when the crisis affects an organization that works in a defined geographic area with a lot of people.

Downside of This Strategy. Many people won't open their doors or will be rude. It is important to make sure the canvassers feel safe and are well trained. Volunteers need to be trustworthy, as they can be carrying a lot of cash by the end of their shift.

House Parties

Income. You can expect to make $1,000 or more for each party.

How It Works. House parties are one of my favorite strategies because they are so malleable and require little staff work. Basically, a loyal fan of your organization invites his or her friends to their house. The invitation makes clear from the beginning that this will be a fundraiser: "Come learn about the important work of It's About Time and what is happening in the world of prison reform. It's About Time is launching a new campaign to change the way prison sentences are determined. Bring your questions and your checkbook."

The host of the party provides refreshments. About halfway through the allotted time of the party, someone from the organization describes the campaign the group is embarked on or simply what the organization does. Ideally, the host, but if necessary another volunteer or a staff person, makes a pitch for donations, the audience writes out their checks, and the party concludes shortly after the money is collected. An added component that is very effective is for the person doing the pitch to ask not only for money but also for two people among the guests to give the next house parties, thus expanding the program.

In the course of three months, an organization could have six to ten parties. Most house parties average twenty to twenty-five people; the average gift is around $40 or $50. A college student throwing a party might only raise $500 from fifty other students; a person with a small apartment might only invite five or six people, but they could raise $1,000. As much as possible, aim for each party raising $1,000. A house party program with ten parties can raise $10,000 or more, plus bring in a world of new donors. Sometimes, wealthier donors invite just a few people who give $1,000 or more each. In that instance, the house party is more of a soirée, and the discussion might go on for several hours.

Upside of This Strategy. This is an easy and inexpensive way to attract new donors and to educate a cross section of people about your issue. It is also a relatively easy and short-term way for someone to help your organization.

Downside of This Strategy. People can promise to do house parties and then keep postponing them, so it is not always a strategy that can be implemented quickly. Sometimes people expect too much of staff in terms of organizing and follow-up, and if not trained and practiced, the host can give a really bad pitch and the party will not raise much money.

Second-Collection Sunday

Income. Expect to make anywhere from $300 to thousands of dollars, depending on the number of congregations involved.

Workers Needed. You'll need one or two congregants for each church that is approached. If someone related to your organization is active in the Council of Churches, this is an easier strategy.

How It Works. People in your organization who belong to a church approach their minister or church board about letting your organization be the recipient of a second collection. After the regular church collection, someone from either the church or your group (or a person affiliated with both) gives a brief pitch and the baskets are passed a second time. You can do this with just one church or you can organize several churches to do it on the same Sunday.

Upside of This Strategy. You are going to an audience of people who are good givers and you can appeal to them all at once. If your constituency is largely faith-based, this is a great way to take advantage of their contacts.

Downside of This Strategy. You can spend a lot of time trying to get just a few places to agree. Sometimes the second collection is not very big.

Dinner Dance

Income. Net can vary from $3,000 to $10,000. This event requires front money for printing, rental of the venue, and deposits for the band or disc jockey and the caterer. It is a more expensive strategy all around than other strategies recommended.

Workers Needed Before the Event. You'll need three or four to plan the event, lay out the tasks, and find other volunteers to do most of the work. These three or four people might also decide on a date and secure a venue.

You'll need three or four more people to put together an adbook. Their job will be selling ads to vendors, larger nonprofits, lawyers, financial planners, and accountants who may want to advertise to a nonprofit audience.

Three or four more people are needed to advertise the event, send out invitations, and handle the details prior to the event.

A week before the event, three or four more people will join the team to handle all details of the night of the event.

Workers Needed the Night of the Event. Most of these people will work the night of the event to make sure it goes smoothly.

Upside of This Strategy. Most volunteers love working on events, and it is easier to get them to work on something like this than on the major donor campaign. It is a good way to train new volunteers and build community among the team. This event attracts people who might not give you money otherwise; it also attracts people who may be interested in your group for whom the event is the entry point.

Downside of This Strategy. Although dinner dances can raise much more money than I have estimated here, they also can cost a lot of money. If you have little front money or don't want to take a big risk, do this on a smaller scale, as described in the following discussion. See if people like it and let the event grow over time.

Variation. Rather than a hotel ballroom, have the event in a community center or school gymnasium, which should be free or low cost to use. Use paper streamers and balloons to make it festive, but don't invest a lot in fancy centerpieces. You can arrange the food to be a competition. People pay a small fee to enter the food competition in different categories, such as main course, salad, or dessert. People who come to the event get a sample of each entry and vote on which they like best. A cash bar can provide extra income, but be sure to comply with any laws about serving alcohol. Dance music can be provided by a local band or local disc jockey who wants to become better known. Ask them for a discounted rate. Advertise the event by word-of-mouth and posters hung in the neighborhood of the event. Ask ten board members to sell ten tickets each at $20 to $35 for a ticket. If successful, you could gross about $7,000 (one hundred people attending at an average of $25 per person, twenty food competitors paying an entry fee of $10 each, and $2,500 or more from the adbook sales). Expenses will include design and printing of the adbook, buying drinks to sell, printing tickets, printing nice-looking certificates for the winners of the food contests, and possibly mailing thank-you notes to volunteers after the event is over. Expenses could be as high as half of the gross, but if you really work on doing this in a grassroots way, getting donations for as many things as possible, you should be able to keep expenses to one-third of the gross.

This is the kind of event that can grow. Here's an example. A dessert competition called Kiss My Sweet, put on by a group with a total annual budget of $250,000, was organized along the lines of the variation just described. By the fourth year the event netted $50,000! As it grew it attracted dessert entries from top chefs from the restaurants in town as well as from lay people entering their favorite brownies or pecan pies.

FOLLOW-UP

All of these events require follow-up. Thank-you notes, records entered into the database, evaluation forms, thank-yous to volunteers—without the infrastructure and commitment to follow up, you might as well skip the strategy altogether. Scattershot follow-up and poor records are the reason that a problem turns into a crisis in many organizations. As you plan these strategies, make sure that appropriate follow-up is in the plans, including a list of follow-up tasks and enough volunteers to get the job done properly.

CREATE YOUR OWN VARIATIONS

The strategies described here are a sampling of possibilities; let them lead you to other ideas. For example, while a PTA trying to keep a school's art and music program going in the face of cuts in public school spending could not do a second-collection Sunday, a privately funded homeless shelter would find that a perfect strategy. However, the idea of one fundraising opportunity happening in several places at the same time leads the PTA to vary the strategy: they go to every art gallery, music store, and nightclub in town and ask each business to donate 5 percent of profits on one day for the school art and music programs. The idea is reported in the local paper and participating businesses experience an uptick in business on that day, making the PTA's 5 percent a nice amount of money and the businesses wanting to help again.

A group working primarily with low-income people may not have good prospects for a major donor program, at least in the short term. However, they start a pledge program instead, recognizing that while their constituents cannot give $250 at once, a goodly cross section of them can give $20 a month. In one organization, five board members committed themselves to finding thirty people to give $25 a month and raised $9,000 in a year—the exact amount that had been cut by the county from their budget. This organization works almost entirely with people earning minimum wage or out of work for whom $25 a month is a steep stretch. These are their major donors.

SETTING PRIORITIES

No group will be able to do every strategy I have suggested, and choosing which ones will work best is tricky. Of course you need money and you don't have much money to spend to raise your money. But keep in mind that as you are coming out of your crisis, you need a team of fundraising volunteers that is beginning to gel and you need to attract donors. As much as possible, choose a cross section of strategies that will do all of these things. You might decide to do a garage sale primarily because it is a low-cost way to raise money, a phone-a-thon because it is a good way to give people practical experience in talking with donors, and a special event such as the dinner dance because it builds a team of volunteers. With the skills that you learn from all three of these strategies, you might feel more ready to launch a major donor campaign. You will have the money for the materials needed, the volunteers trained to ask for money, and the knowledge of how to create a team. At the end of that experience, you will have more money, more volunteers who are sophisticated and trained, and a lot of practice perfecting your message and learning what people who are making a big investment in your organization really want to know.

THE PROCESS OF CHOOSING STRATEGIES

For the first year after your crisis begins to be resolved, put together a fundraising plan at the beginning of each quarter. You can plan for longer time periods, but focus on the details quarter by quarter. That way, as you learn and evaluate, you can change your plans accordingly. First, determine how many volunteers and what kind of volunteers you are going to need. If you have a development director or other staff person in charge of fundraising, that person's job is to recruit a chair for each of the strategies. That chair, with help, will recruit an ad hoc committee that includes all the workers needed. Keep in mind that people who enjoy working at yard sales are different from people who are willing to work the phones, and that people willing to ask for large amounts of money may not be interested in either selling at a yard sale or phoning. Because you are using these strategies to build your fundraising team, try to expand your volunteer crew for each one, so that you do not have very many overlapping volunteers.

Think widely as you recruit. In one organization, teenagers were used for the phone-a-thon, recruited from a high school sociology class that needed to do some community service as part of their course work. The teens loved being together, they learned quickly, and they raised a lot of money. In another organization, a board member whose mother likes going to yard sales asked her mother to help; her mother brought along three of her friends. They priced the items quickly because they knew the market. One woman pulled out some fine antique dinnerware and sold it to an antique dealer for much more money than it would have brought at the garage sale. They had a great time.

By building your plan around flexible ad hoc committees, you can bring in all kinds of people who are willing to help briefly and you can play to people's interests and strengths.

A CRITICAL TIME

The period of time between the end of the crisis and the end of the post-crisis healing is a critical one. It is a great time to begin to develop a culture of recruiting a lot of volunteers for intensive, short assignments, and for learning about your organizational capacities to attract donors using various strategies. The crisis is a time to really change organizational culture. It is important that in the post-crisis period you don't drift back into bad habits, such as letting fundraising become a one- or two-person activity or gradually letting go of high-touch elements in your fundraising.

I hope you are realizing that coming at this problem with the idea that your *only* choice is to raise money ironically gives you a lot of choices. Cutting back simply leads to more cutting back. When you really move into the principle of fundraising, you become much more creative, outgoing, and resourceful.

CHAPTER 8

Fundraising Strategies with Long-Term Payoff

Once you have bought some time by raising some money from your inner circle of supporters using face-to-face or other personal asking and you are implementing your plan to get through the next six to twelve months, you need to begin or expand using fundraising strategies that will provide stability for your organization over time.

The strategies that will be most helpful to you over the long term are any that help build a strong individual donor base and that do not require a lot of front money. Such strategies include personal solicitation (face-to-face, phone, or personal letter), small-scale direct mail, certain kinds of special events, pledge programs, bequest programs, Web site and other Internet fundraising, and some earned-income strategies. If you have more than one hundred donors, skip the section called "Starting from Scratch" and go to "Best Ways to Work with Current Donors." "Starting from Scratch" is for organizations with fewer than one hundred individual donors. This chapter concludes with a look at some possible earned-income strategies.

WHY DEVELOP A BROAD BASE OF INDIVIDUAL DONORS

A caveat before we begin: If the only reason you are moving toward having a donor base is that you can't get foundation funding anymore, you won't be very successful. If you think that when the economy recovers and foundation funding goes up again (as it will eventually) you will get back on the foundation wagon and make grants your main source of income, then you might as well scale back and wait for that day. Someday there will be a lot of foundation funding again, and then, some other day, there won't. That is the nature of foundation funding. It is designed to help start or expand programs and experiment with new ways of doing things, but it is not designed and never will be good for providing the ongoing costs of doing business.

You need to see a broad base of individual donors not only as the one place where you can continue to raise money now, but also as a test of community support; a source of ideas, volunteers, and bigger and bigger donations; and a pool of ambassadors educating the public in the form of their friends and colleagues about the issues your organization addresses. A broad base of donors has intrinsic value and is something to pursue whatever the economy, the government, or foundations are doing.

STARTING FROM SCRATCH

When I was a child, there was a column in a women's magazine called "Can This Marriage Be Saved?" The column responded to letters, most from women, who would write in with tales of spouses who were cold and unfeeling, adulterous, compulsive gamblers, out of work, depressed, and so on. An ever-optimistic counselor would give two paragraphs of advice and—presto!—the column was over. Occasionally people would write that, indeed, applying the advice given had saved their marriage. When organizations in nearly impossible situations call me for advice, I often feel like that counselor. Fortunately, I usually can go beyond two paragraphs in my advice, and I keep in mind that the word "nearly" is key in the notion of "nearly impossible." Those organizations starting with few or no donors and no earned income have a steep learning curve and may have to make some temporary cuts in their programs as they figure out a different way to raise money. Some won't make it. But some will. You might as well plan to be in the latter group.

By this point, your crisis task force should have already had some success finding a few donors who have given you enough money to get through the next few months. Many of these donors may be other activists, relatives of staff and board members, and in general people who do not wish to make a long-term commitment to your organization but were just helping out.

Now you need to look for people who believe in the work of your organization. Having completed the work in Chapter Four on the message, you should be very clear about your case and your message.

Here's a not-so-secret fact about fundraising: people know people like themselves. If a person enjoys listening to public radio and can give $50 to their local station, he or she will know ten other people who also listen to public radio and can also give $50. That person will also know two or three people who could give $100. What you have to do with every person who gives you any amount is to ask them who else they know who can help you. Some people will help you in this way and some won't. Sometimes you will ask for more contacts right away and sometimes you will wait until you know the person better. You will also have to find out how the contacts of your donors like to be contacted themselves.

Now is the time to put this bit of knowledge to use. Make three lists of people:

1. Who would be really upset, almost devastated, if your organization closed? List twenty people by name and note what type of people they are: clients? volunteers? parents? union members? lawyers? teachers? clergy? Every organization will have a slightly different list. Don't reject a name because you think the person has no money to give. We will cross that bridge later.

2. Who would be sad if your organization closed but not as upset as the people in the first group? Again, list twenty names and what type of people they are.

3. Finally, who would be annoyed, inconvenienced, or momentarily sad? Make another list of twenty.

Some people in the first category may have already served on the crisis task force and may have already contributed money. The Crisis Task Force members should be asked if they are willing to keep on helping in a lower-key way. Those who have helped financially should be asked if they know other people who have never given who would be interested in supporting the organization. In many organizations, people in this first category do not have much money but they do have friends and colleagues. If they generate ten or twenty names each and two or three of those contacts do the same, you could be recruiting a dozen or more donors each week.

Here's an example. In one organization, two volunteers worked with a staff person to develop a donor base. They identified twenty people who fit the description of the first list and asked them for names of others who could give. Ten of these people each supplied ten names of people they thought could give $25, $50, $100, or more. The organization generated personalized letters to these hundred people (in this case, personalized means opening the letter with "Dear Mr. Jones" rather than "Dear Friend," and beginning with a sentence such as, "Your friend, Mary Smith, gave me your name . . ."). In the first week, one hundred letters went out; in the second week, ten gifts came in. Those ten people were thanked by the people who had given the name in the first place. They were also asked if they could think of other people who would give. Four of the ten gave a total of fifty names among them. Those letters went out and ten more gifts came in. In the meantime, one of the original twenty people, excited by the response she was generating, asked more friends for more names and brought in another hundred names. In the first few weeks, the organization sent five hundred personalized first-class letters and brought in sixty-five new donors and $2,600, plus one gift of $2,500. The donor who gave $2,500 was contacted and agreed to host a small party at her house, which raised another $5,000 from five other people. Over the course of two years of systematic, if somewhat tedious, work, the organization built a base of donors from twenty people to one thousand and built an income stream from $300 to $75,000. Every donor was asked for more names. By sending personalized letters with first-class stamps, the group generated a response rate of 7.5

percent overall. In the process, they found one hundred people who gave $250 or more, including the person who gave $2,500. It took a lot of work on the part of the two volunteers with the support of the staff person. However, if this group keeps up their "high-touch" fundraising, they should be able to raise more money in less time each year.

When I tell stories like this, I always hear, "Well, good for that group, but no one in our group knows anyone who could give $2,500." But what you have to realize is that you don't know who everyone in your group knows. People often surprise themselves at who they know when they really put their mind to it. The point is to keep at it and not to get discouraged by the people who choose either not to give money themselves or provide other names.

What you will often notice is that the people on the first list start pulling in people from the second list. However, the people on the second list should be asked to open doors to larger groups of people. They often have supported your organization because they would support any organization working on the issue you are working on or because they have a general belief in your work. They are usually not personally affected by what you do and they are generally not personally involved. This means they move in other circles and they can help you branch out. Perhaps they can get you invited to their Rotary Club or give you access to their union members. They may be willing to bring your organization to their house of worship for a second collection or for a donation from the "domestic missions budget" or something similar.

In either list, some people will be able to lead you to other people, one person at a time, and some will be able to get your organization in front of a group of people—a house party, a service club, a bar association, a conference. You need to take advantage of any opportunity because you don't know where it will lead.

The third list includes people who have received income from you, such as landlords, computer salespeople, restaurant owners, or conference center managers, as well as people who have received useful information, pithy quotes, or great stories from your organization's work, such as researchers, journalists, and politicians. If you are a rehabilitation program or the like this list also includes employers of your clients. People on this list may help you with a donation and should be offered that opportunity, but they can also help you raise money from other institutions—small businesses, corporations, professional associations. They may also help you figure out an earned-income strategy.

Here's an example. An organization providing a range of services for homeless people has a program that helps formerly homeless people learn how to interview for a job. They help with résumé preparation and teach interviewing skills. In coalition with another organization, they provide clothing for job interviews and, for those who get a job, two weeks' worth of clothing to wear to work. Several corporations that have found reliable workers through this program often call this group when they have jobs available.

Now this organization has lost half of its city funding. A corporate executive on the third list suggests that they offer résumé-writing and interviewing skills to the community for a small fee. She offers a meeting room in her office building where they can hold the class. With unemployment skyrocketing, the organization finds it is not hard to fill the classes. People pay on a sliding scale from $10 to $250. Those who get jobs often make an additional donation. The organization expands its repertoire to new college graduates and has now been asked to teach this course as part of the community college's adult school curriculum. The classes themselves bring in a small but steady income stream, and more important, the graduates now form the basis of the organization's donors. The group has expanded its donor base from one hundred people giving $1,500 to two hundred people giving $15,000 in just one year. Their classes in the first year bring in an additional $30,000 gross, and net about $20,000. This will not fully replace their city funding, but it has been a relatively easy strategy to put in place.

Sometimes, people in the third category help you raise money by helping you save money. I've heard of several instances in which landlords, fearful of being unable to rent their space, lowered the rent or gave an organization one month's rent free. In one instance a landlord canceled the rent for six months while the organization put its new fundraising programs in place.

People in this category can also help your financial condition in other ways. A service club donated the proceeds from their annual pancake breakfast to one organization. A specialist in marketing on the Web offered to volunteer for another organization as Webmaster for one year. He spiffed up the site, continues to change it so it is fun to visit, registered the organization with a wide range of search engines, and got them set up to take credit cards on the Web. They are beginning to see the fruits of that effort, with their Web income doubling every quarter. It is now at $40,000 a year. Two volunteers from the original Crisis Task Force have started a monthly e-mail newsletter, which drives more traffic to the Web site.

As you can see, building a base of donors from scratch is a slog. However, not having money is a drag, so choose: slog or drag? I hope you will choose slog because individual donor fundraising gets easier as you go along and grows geometrically. It is stable and secure and after you get the hang of it, it can be fun.

BEST WAYS TO WORK WITH CURRENT DONORS

Many organizations that formed in the late 1970s and 1980s started with individual donors; as foundation or government funding became more available, the organizations neglected those donors. Having a donor is not like having a pillowcase or a table. Donors take maintenance. They are living, breathing beings with feelings and attitudes, and they are being sought by 1.5 million other nonprofits. Certainly, they gravitate to organizations they believe in, but if they have a choice between two groups they believe in and one pays attention to them and one doesn't, it is not hard to guess where they will go. So a donor base is perhaps more like a garden—there is always something to be done and the garden will do best when tended. There are three major areas of maintaining your donors that I will cover in this section: know how they want to be treated, keep them informed, and encourage them to leave you some money after they are gone.

First, Segment Your Donors

High-touch fundraising means fundraising from people in a way they like. Almost everyone appreciates thoughtful personal attention, so we give such attention to all our donors as best we can. But people also have individual likes and dislikes; to the extent that we can accommodate these, we must. If someone sends you $35 with a note that says "Please only ask me once a year," you should be able to code this donor in your database so that their name is suppressed for any other mailing during that year. That person will not be invited to an event or get the spring appeal. Similarly, someone who writes on their reply card "Absolutely no phone calls" is never phoned. This information is noted in their donor record. In fact, even if you have recorded their phone number from the information on their check, don't enter it into your database. If you don't have it, you are much less likely to make a mistake and call.

Most donors, however, don't tell us directly what they want. Nonetheless, they may indicate their preferences by their behavior. What we want to do is make an informed guess about their behavior before they decide not to give us money anymore. Segmenting, which means dividing the donors into smaller batches according to various criteria, allows you to take their preferences into account and saves your organization time and money because you are not directing strategies to people who have never responded to them.

In all this I am assuming you have a good database, which is a dangerous and often false assumption. But I would say this: Even if you have to stand on the street and ask for money, find the funds to buy a decent database. There are many very adequate databases specifically designed for fundraising; the least expensive cost about $90. (You may be able to get a "free" database, but it may not be worth more than you paid for it.) You should not need to spend more than $2,500 for an excellent database, not including technical support, which should not break your bank either. When considering a database, make sure it can provide some basic functions, as shown in the sidebar. (See Resources for more on fundraising systems.)

What a Good Database Should Do.

For every donor:

- Full name, correctly spelled with preferred title (Mr., Ms., Dr., Your Holiness, and so on)
- Current address where donor prefers to receive mail
- Date, source, and amount of first gift
- Date, source, and amount of every subsequent gift
- Additional involvement in your organization (such as board member, activist, vendor)
- Whether donor responds to written appeals more than once a year
- Whether donor responds to telephone appeals
- Whether you may exchange or rent donor's name and address

Additional information about major donors and major donor prospects:

- Family (including name of spouse or partner and children)
- Additional work or home addresses
- Special programmatic interests
- Likes or dislikes that affect raising money from this donor
- Other organizations this donor supports: how, and how much
- Names of people in your organization able to contact this donor personally
- History of all contact with this donor

Additional information you may wish to track about all or a subset of your donors:

- Willingness to volunteer
- Naming our group in their will
- Contacts this donor has that may be helpful to us

The first set of segments you should create is very simple. Donors should be sorted by *size* of gift, *longevity* of giving, and *frequency* of giving.

Size. Determine what amount of money is more than most people in your constituency can give and create a list of donors who give that much or more. In some organizations, this may be $100, but for most it will probably be $250 and up.

Longevity. This is the most important variable—those who have stayed with you for three or more years. Create a category for those people. If you are an old organization and your records are very good, you may want to create other categories of those who have given for five or more years, or even for ten or more years.

Frequency. While there are many donors who only give once a year, there are many others who give every time they are asked. Create a category for those who give two or more times a year.

Print out a list of people who have given $100 or more (in one gift) for three or more years. Note which of those people also give more than once a year. Your personal solicitation efforts should be directed at this group. They care about you and have shown that caring for several years. Show this list to trusted board members, volunteers, and people who know your community and who have some discretion. See if they know whether any of the people on this list are capable of giving a lot more. Perhaps Jane Smith gives you $250 a year and has done so for three years. A volunteer knows that Jane Smith gives $1,000 to an organization similar to yours and this volunteer says that Jane has spoken very highly of both organizations. As a general rule, donors should be asked to upgrade their gift every two years anyway, so Jane is a little overdue.

Donors who only give once a year should only be asked once or twice a year, whereas those who give every time they are asked might get an extra appeal during the year or be asked to join a pledge program. Those who always renew by phone will no longer get three renewal letters before being phoned, but instead will get one renewal letter followed by a phone call. By

Fundraising in Times of Crisis

observing patterns among your donors, you can save yourself a lot of time and money and increase your fundraising income with very little extra work on your part.

In addition to size, longevity, and frequency of gifts, begin to make other categories. Note which donors only come to events, or perhaps only come to one event. They should not get regular appeal letters unless you have evidence that they give to appeal letters as well. If, for example, a donor only gives when she comes to your signature event, does so for three years or more, and does not give to anything else, that is a sign that she does not need to get the other appeal letters. If that donor does not come to the event one year, then she can get a letter after the event telling how well the event did and how she was missed and asking for a contribution. Note which donors only give to appeals for specific things (playgrounds, scholarships, capital projects) and who do not send money to general appeals. If you have a specific need, pull out these donors and approach them more personally for that need. These are often your best prospects for capital campaigns.

Identify the people who give several times a year and either add one more appeal to them or see if you can convert them to monthly or quarterly donors by inviting them to become members of a pledge club.

Our goal in doing this segmenting is threefold: we will give donors the kind of attention they want; we will save ourselves from getting phone calls or letters from frustrated donors saying, "You send too much mail," or "I can't stand being phoned," or "You are using all the money I gave you to ask me for more money"; and, our main purpose, we will be able to focus our primary fundraising energy on donors who are loyal to the organization itself rather than to a person in the organization or an event. We appreciate all gifts and all motives for giving. But our best chance of getting a donation year in and year out is by building a relationship with the donor—a relationship that transcends any of the people in the group and that continues through any number of changes the group may go through.

Let me explain further. Someone who is new to fundraising will tend to focus on finding donors who "have money." They will say, "I don't know anyone who has money," or "My brother-in-law has money so I should ask him." Their sole criteria for identifying prospective donors is their ability to give. As soon as people learn that what a person *has* and what they will *give* are all but unrelated, they move to the next level of understanding fundraising. People are fascinated by the studies that show that Mississippi, one of the poorest states in the nation, has the highest per capita rate of giving of any state, or that people with incomes of less than $10,000 give away a higher percentage of their income than people with incomes of $100,000 or more.

One element that distinguishes those who have money from those who give money is that those who give generally do so because of a personal relationship to the asker. Consider this fact: when people are asked to remember the last donation they made and why they made it, 80 percent of them will say "Someone asked me," but only 50 percent of that group can remember on what organization's behalf the asking was done. People do give to causes, but they are more likely to make significant gifts to causes that involve people they know.

In the early stages of individual asking, people new to fundraising are likely to ask all their friends for money, and they are likely to have success. Through house parties, personal letters, and phone calls, a team of people will build a donor base. If an organization stays at this learning level, however, they will have a lot of donors whose loyalty is not to the organization but to a person in the organization. When that person leaves, the donors leave also.

So now we must move to the next level of understanding who prospects are, and that is to look for very clear evidence of belief in the cause. People will often say, "But my friends do believe in the cause—that is partly why we are friends. We have values in common." Certainly that is true. But we have to look closer at our friends because all of us care about far more things than we can give money to. We all know organizations that we hope someone will support. We believe in them, we think our community is a better place because of them, but we do not give our money to them because our charitable dollars are directed elsewhere. Most people who give to nonprofits give to between five and fifteen organizations. Some people support as many as thirty or forty organizations. But almost anyone cares about far more than forty issues. So we are looking for donors who will place our organization and our cause on the list they give money to, regardless of who is involved as long as they have confidence in the good work of the organization. We focus our upgrading and intensive renewal energy on those folks. Some people are loyal enough to our cause, but they really love an event that we do. We focus on getting them to keep coming to the event and on adding income streams to the event rather than appealing to them several times a year by mail when all they ever give to is the event.

Let's look at an example. Mary is very involved in Feral Cat Rescue. This all-volunteer organization captures feral cats in the community where she lives, has them spayed or neutered and vaccinated, and tries to tame and place the kittens, returning the older cats that can't be domesticated back into the wild. For some reason, her town is known for its kindness to cats and a lot of cats get dumped there. Mary spends most of her evenings and weekends working for this group, as does a core group of ten other volunteers. Their fundraising has provided money for live traps and educational materials, and for reimbursing veterinarians for medicines and other expenses beyond the services they donate. The group's dream is to get a mobile van where they could both treat cats and display those ready for adoption at shopping malls. To fulfill this dream, they need to raise about $50,000 a year in operating expense; the van will be a major capital expense of $30,000, followed by upkeep expenses.

Mary and her friends have built an impressive donor list by asking all their friends and friends' friends for money. But they notice that the donors tend to keep giving at the $25 and $35 level; no amount of asking seems to move them up. Feral Cat Rescue also has a lower rate of donor retention than is healthy—about 55 percent (a healthy rate is 66 percent). A handful of donors give more and some give very major gifts of $2,500 and $5,000, which is how they are able to do as much as they do. Mary approaches me for help in upgrading her donors, and we quickly realize the problem. Mary has a lot of donors who like and admire her and probably like cats, but who are not really that loyal to this cause. As we go through the list, I ask her and her volunteers whether they know the favorite causes of the donors to Feral Cat Rescue. The answers are illuminating: "peace in the Middle East," "the local repertory theater," "music programs in the schools," "civil liberties." Very few of their donors even give significantly to the environment, and none of them seem to give to other animal rescue or animal rights organizations.

With this information, I suggest the group think about their donors as falling into three categories:

Those who are primarily loyal to the event

Those who will always give something but will not increase their giving

Those who might make Feral Cat Rescue one of their top giving priorities

Then I suggest they create a committee of people from their most loyal and committed donors whose job it will be to recruit more of the same. Mary and her friends have already cast a wide net and hauled in everybody they knew. Now it is time to take that broad base and work with a small cross section of people who might give more. They identify from their donor list twenty people who have given $250 or more each year for three years and ask them to come to a fundraising brainstorming meeting. The letter reads,

Dear Name of Donor,

You have helped Feral Cat Rescue for the past several years. We are so grateful, and even though cats don't show gratitude, in their own way our rescued feline friends are grateful too.

Today I am not writing to ask you for money but for a different kind of help. You are one of our most loyal donors and we need more people like you. As you know from our newsletter, we want to buy a mobile van where we can treat the cats and show those that are available for adoption. To do this, we need to ramp up our fundraising efforts.

Would you do me a great favor and come to a meeting to help us brainstorm the best ways to raise money? We need the help of our community in thinking through various ideas we have and in getting more ideas.

I promise the following:

- There will be good food.
- The meeting will only last two hours.
- We will have pictures of our latest rescues on the wall.
- We will have fun.
- We will not ask you for money at this meeting and there is no obligation to come to future meetings.

Your presence will make a big difference. I'll call you in a few days to answer questions and see if you can come.

Best wishes,

Mary Catlady

Seven people come to the meeting. All agree that expanding the donor base is a good idea. They feel there are two issues the group has to attend to: Feral Cat Rescue is not that well known and those who do know about it probably have no idea how much the organization costs because it is known as an all-volunteer group.

Five people pledge to help generate names of potential donors and do other work. After six months, one of them has gotten the mailing list of their area's subscribers to cat magazines and is sending a letter to those people; another has put together a list of people who have adopted a cat from Feral Cat Rescue but who are not on the donor list, and is calling them; and the other three are approaching their own friends, but with the intention of looking for people who really care about this issue.

The people who mostly give out of loyalty and respect for Mary or her friends are still asked, but only once a year, and there is no attempt to upgrade them. They are renewing at a higher rate than they have in the past.

By being more systematic with their donors and clarifying who was loyal to what, Feral Cat Rescue is able to raise more money and focus their upgrading efforts on people who care about feral cats rather than people who care mostly about Mary and her friends.

To get further clarity about who your supporters are, it is helpful to make a list of types of people who support your organization and their possible reasons for doing so. Think about the different motives people have for giving and see where your group fits. You will notice that some people will give because they share your philosophy. They think your approach to the issue is the correct one. Others will give because they have been personally touched by the work of the group or know someone who has. Others will give because they are community minded and think that your group is a good addition to the community.

People can be in all these categories and many more. But going back to Feral Cat Rescue, George and Monica give because they love the fat tabby they got from the rescue. They do not have strong opinions about spay-and-neuter clinics. In fact, they are mostly involved in the arts. Esmeralda gives although she has no cats. She cares about birds, particularly those that nest on the ground, and wants to protect them from feral cats. She wishes the cats would all find loving homes, but mostly wants to keep them from breeding. Harry and Carl have just retired to this community. They have always supported groups working with and for animals wherever they have lived and give money to national animal rights organizations as well. They have two dogs and are actually not cat people, but they give anyway. Amina is a veterinarian and gives both time and money. Insofar as these people represent a cross section of people like them, each should be treated differently. Harry and Carl, who don't have cats, may well be better major donor prospects than George and Monica, who do, because Harry and Carl care about this cause. Esmeralda will be a good person to lead the group to other people who care about the specific project of the spay-and-neuter program.

In times of economic downturn or world instability, loyal donors are both the bread-and-butter and the lifeblood, to mix metaphors, for an organization. Whatever work you can do to build your group of loyal donors is critical. Matching strategies with types of donors will help build loyalty.

Of course asking for money, even in a way the donor responds to, cannot be the only way you are in touch with donors. You need to be telling the donors what you do and helping them be ambassadors of your work with their own friends. Examine all your dealings with donors and make sure everything you do is having the effect you want.

Second, Keep Donors Informed

Examine how you are keeping donors informed about your work. The main vehicles for this communication are your newsletter, your annual report, and your Web site.

The newsletter. The first thing to be examined should be the newsletter. So often, a newsletter is slapped together with little thought about who is reading it and what will they think about it. The newsletter should contain a balance of articles that either inform (as oppose to overwhelm), touch the heart, or make the donor pleased with the organization and happy to be a giver. More and more it seems that donors care less about having their names listed in the newsletter and more about getting information, or even having a shorter newsletter. Anything that can convince the donor that their money is well spent will be worth the space. Profiles of board members and stories about donors are always useful for pulling in more people. Short stories about your work with reference to a longer version on your Web site will drive traffic to your site and allow those interested to find out more without overwhelming those who are satisfied with the CliffsNotes.

You may want to consider having fewer paper newsletters and using e-mail newsletters for short and more frequent contact. Some organizations give donors a choice of paper or e-mail newsletters, but e-mail is a different medium than paper. E-mail newsletters should be short and pasted into the body of the e-mail, not downloaded. E-mail newsletters can also give a short story that links to a Web page. A paper newsletter as short as an e-mail one will seem skimpy. An e-mail newsletter as long as a paper one will seem overwhelming. E-mail lends itself to text and not graphics. You can't take your e-mail newsletter with you to the backyard to read, but it also doesn't get lost in a pile. Because of the different functions of e-mail and paper newsletters, most groups find that combining them works well. Environmental groups with donors who are computer users find that donors appreciate an e-mail-only newsletter as more environmental, whereas a group with a lot of senior citizens may experience some resistance to e-mail. About 75 percent of American families own a computer and most people have access to one, but you will want to know how accessible e-mail is for your audience. As computers become even more commonly used, you will need to reexamine this question often.

Annual reports. An annual report is another opportunity for building loyalty or boring the donor. Fancy and expensive-looking annual reports are out for the time being, which ironically makes the report more difficult to design. It has to be readable and accessible without looking expensive. Pictures are still important, but can be in black and white. Captions can be used to tell whole stories. Financial information should be explained, not just copied from the audit. Donors do not know how to interpret this information and a friendly page from the treasurer of the board will go a long way to reassuring them that money is well spent.

Web site. People often think of a Web site as mainly a way of recruiting new donors. This is an important function and the site should be built with that in mind. However, a Web site is also a great donor retention strategy. You can drive donors to your site by reminding them of the site in every piece of correspondence. Put your Web address everywhere. In your letters to donors, refer to them to your Web site for more information. Your newsletter and e-mail newsletter should always refer people to your site. Make sure your site is linked to those of other groups like yours and that it is registered with search engines. Try to find your site from other organizations' sites by typing your name or your issue into search engines.

For most organizations, the Web does not provide a big income stream right now, but it is the up-and-coming way of being in touch with the public and you will want to get ahead of the curve on this strategy. There are many volunteers who dislike asking for money in person but enjoy working on a Web site. It is generally not hard to find people who will help with the site but, like all volunteer work, their efforts need to be part of the larger picture.

Third, Consider a Bequest Program

The ultimate gift from a donor is a planned gift, where the full receipt of the gift is deferred until the death of the donor. For someone to pledge you money through a planned gift, they need to believe in your organization in a deep way. They must believe the organization will always be needed and will continue to do great work indefinitely, and they must believe you will use their gift wisely. There are many forms of planned giving, but the one groups should start with (and for many organizations, there is no need to do more) is a bequest program.

To make a bequest to your group, a person simply notes in their will what property they wish your organization to have. People who already have a will and don't wish to rewrite it can add a codicil or amendment to the will specifying a gift to your organization.

Bequests are the most common form of planned gifts; even so, they are not that common. About 60 percent of Americans die without a will; of those people who make a will, only about 8 percent leave money to charity.

You can start a bequest program simply by putting a small notice in your newsletter and on your Web site: "As you are making out your will, please remember us with a bequest. Our full legal name is _____ and our full address is _____." Or "If you have provided for (name of your group) in your estate plans, please let us know. If not, please let us show you how you can. Write for our free brochure." (Be sure you have a free brochure.)

Direct most of your bequest information to all the donors who are in your *longevity* category. Don't worry so much about their age. None of us knows when we will be called from this life, and everyone should have a will. The donors who have a will who are most likely to include your organization in it are the ones who have been giving you money for several years.

EARNED INCOME

Another source of revenue to consider is earned income. About 50 percent of nonprofit income nationally is money from the sale of products, fees, rents—anything that does not come from direct donor gifts or funder grants. It is beyond the scope of this book to describe all the ways your organization might consider earning income, but it is worth your time to think about what your organization knows, what it provides for free, and what it can create, and see if any of these skills or activities can be commercialized. Earned income can require a lot of front money, but it doesn't have to. Similarly, a focus on earning income can take groups away from mission, but it doesn't have to.

Let's look at a couple of examples. An organization works with twelve- to fifteen-year-old kids who have had a brush with the law. Every summer they give twenty kids a three-week camping experience that focuses on self-esteem, developing discipline, and teamwork. (They have room for thirty students, but funding for only twenty.) In the winter, they provide counseling in several schools to students who are identified as "at risk." They have always worked with very-low-income students, and their services have always been free. They have a very good reputation. Their work is entirely funded by a government grant. The group has never raised money beyond their grant, believing that their organization's success would spare them from cuts. When they receive word that their funding will be cut by half, they are devastated and completely ill-prepared. They have not kept the names of their alumni; when parents have offered to give money, they have turned it down. When parents have actually sent money, they have not thanked them nor kept a record of the donors' names.

They form a Crisis Task Force, which fortunately includes someone with business skills. He points out that he and a number of other parents like him are worried about their kids and would like to get them into a program like this, but haven't been able to find one. He could afford to pay; so could others. The organization decides to allow ten paying students in addition to the twenty students who come for free. A parent on the Crisis Task Force feels that having some paying full fare and the rest coming for free will create a bad dynamic among the kids; he suggests that everyone pay something. A quick survey of parents shows they would be willing to pay a reasonable fee. So, inside a span of two weeks, the organization adopts a sliding scale of $50 to $2,000, depending on income and using an honor system where each family determines their rate. In the first year, no one pays

Fundraising in Times of Crisis

$50 and no one pays $2,000. People pay anywhere from $100 to $1,500. The organization observes that the camp now has more of a mixed class and mixed race attendance, which improves the experience for the students. In addition, the extra money allows the group to run the camp twice in the summer. Three years later, the group serves sixty kids at the camp and charges a voluntary fee for their counseling services at the schools. These fees have enabled them to hire more counselors and serve more schools. They now have more money than when they depended solely on the government, and they are beginning to build a donor base of people who believe in their program. Their earned income is completely mission-driven and has actually worked in favor of their program.

Here's another example. The workers at a social service agency serving mostly low-income Mexican immigrants notice that at least an hour each day is taken up with someone dropping by who needs a document translated. Since part of this group's mission is to be accessible and available to their constituents, a worker drops what he or she is doing and translates. The group is heavily dependent on foundations, and when they lose a large foundation grant, though they are not yet in crisis, they can see the tidal wave coming. They decide to start a translation service out of their storefront office. They suggest a rate based on the number of pages that must be translated and the technical difficulty of the translation, but people can pay less if they need to. The group hires two well-educated bilingual immigrants as the on-site translators. One is able to serve almost all the drop-ins and the other serves a new clientele that the translation service now brings in: businesses, including realtors, bankers, and others who are willing to pay for these needed services. During the first six months, the service only breaks even, but it frees up the rest of the staff to do their other work. After a year, the translation service begins to show a profit; eventually it provides about 10 percent of the organization's income. Like all good earned-income ventures, some of the people who come in for translation later become donors to the organization as they learn more about what it does.

An earned-income program is not something to enter lightly. You can lose money, you have to know the laws about business-related income, and you can be pulled off mission. But when it works, as in these two examples and others throughout this book, earned income can be a reliable source of funds.

CONCLUSION

It is your organization's job to shift its culture from having one or two sources of money and two or three people raising it to a diversity of sources and people to draw from. By being strategic and methodical, and by involving a lot of different people in various short- and longer-term fundraising tasks, you can make this organizational shift.

CHAPTER 9

Permanent Course Correction

As soon as you feel you have achieved some financial stability, which means you have money in the pipeline or solid plans for raising enough to take you through the next six months, you will want to analyze your fundraising program further, continuing to make changes and concretizing changes you have already made. I say "want to analyze" rather than "need to analyze" because this analysis is more fun and will feel more proactive than what you have been doing up to now. This analysis, coupled with what you have learned so far, will enable you to decide what permanent changes you will be making in your fundraising to face the future more confidently. The analysis can be done over a period of time and it can be done piecemeal.

As you read this chapter and begin identifying elements you want to incorporate into your fundraising, set priorities for the changes you need to make. You can't make them all at once, and it is possible that you can't make some of them for quite a while. You will also become aware of other changes that must be made in your organization, unrelated to fundraising, before more dramatic change in your fundraising can occur. Remember, our purpose is to help your organization not only get through your crisis or avoid the crises that have been described here, but also change its way of fundraising to the extent you need to, so that you will not lurch into another crisis in a few years. Similar to the health world's injunction that you don't need to go on a diet so much as you need to change your relationship to food, what I have been proposing in this book is that you need to change your relationship to how your organization raises money in order to solve present crises and avert future ones.

LOOK AT YOUR FUNDRAISING OVERALL

In addition to looking at the diversity of your funding, as we have talked about, look also at whether your sources of funding are likely to sustain your organization for years to come. A broad base of individual donors recruited using a variety of strategies, along with an income-generation program (the size and scope of which will vary with the group), gives an organization maximum stability and flexibility and enables the group to stay completely focused on mission.

Only a small number of organizations can count on foundations as an ongoing source of major revenue. Government funding *should* be stable, but it is not. In the future, when government officials are actually elected by the majority of the people and government funds are used for programs that benefit the majority of the people and improve the quality of life, government funding will become an important part of many organizations' budgets. In the meantime, public funding is not reliable and may require many compromises in mission even when it is available.

Your goal, then, is to expand those sources of funding that are both expandable and reliable. In the previous chapter we discussed segmenting donors, looking for prospects who believe in your cause, and building a team of people who will work to raise the money you need.

Here are some further things you need to do.

LOOK AT THE RIGHT NUMBERS

All too often, a development director reports that a mail appeal "made $5,000" or a phone-a-thon "netted $3,500." They are surprised to learn that

Fundraising in Times of Crisis

these numbers by themselves are almost meaningless. What is meaningful is to compare the percentage of your response to what you might have expected. This is most easily seen in mail appeals. For example, a mail appeal sent to a list of good prospects who have not given before should yield a 1 percent response. If your organization raised $5,200 from an appeal, your response may or may not be 1 percent. A staff person's grandmother who received the letter and wanted to be supportive of her grandson may have sent $5,000. In that case, though you have a generous new major donor, your appeal would be a major flop. Acting as though that appeal was a success will lead you to send the same package again; that would probably be a mistake.

To obtain the true percentage of response, you divide the number of gifts received by the number of attempts made. For example, if you send one thousand letters by bulk mail, here's what you can expect: some of them don't arrive at all, some are addressed to people who no longer live at that address, many are thrown out without being read, some are read and then thrown out, and a tiny number elicit a gift. Similarly, if you conduct a phone-a-thon you will find that some numbers are blocked, others are disconnected, many people aren't home, many people you do reach don't give, and a handful do.

The following sections tell you what you can reasonably expect from each of your strategies and give you a baseline to determine how your organization compares with the average.

Acquisition

Acquiring new donors is critical for expanding the donor base and replacing donors who drop out. Any strategy can be used to acquire donors, although mail is the most common and the easiest for reaching large numbers of people.

Mail: To a list of people who give money to a cause like yours, with no personalization and sent at bulk mail rates: 1 percent response.

If you send the mailing first class, you can often improve your rate enough to cover the cost difference between first-class and bulk mailing rates and you will have acquired that many more donors. In very small mailings of fewer than a thousand pieces, you can target your list to warmer prospects enough to raise your response to 3 percent and sometimes more. You should always plan on just getting a 1 percent to 2 percent response, though, so that you don't overestimate your income projections.

If you personalize the letters, especially by adding a hand-written personal note in the case of names given to you by board members or other volunteers, you can move your rate of response to 5 percent and sometimes more.

E-newsletter: There are no reliable data on e-newsletters as yet, but there is a fair amount of anecdotal information. Organizations that maintain a regular and useful e-newsletter have found that their subscribers will respond to appeals in the e-newsletter. Sometimes the percentage is actually higher than from direct mail. However, it is not advisable to do fundraising with e-mail addresses of people who have not asked to be on your e-list. You don't want your group associated with e-mail "spam."

Phone: Calling a list of people who give to a similar organization but not to yours: 5 percent response.

Again, personalizing the phone call by having board members call friends or by being allowed to use someone's name in making a call will raise your percentage of response by 5 percent or 10 percent.

Door-to-door canvass: Sending trained volunteers (or, more expensively, paid canvassers) into residential neighborhoods: 12 percent of households will give something. Often the gift is a small cash gift, but it is a start. Sending volunteers into their own neighborhoods will raise the percentage of response.

Any of the acquisition strategies described so far, when done in combination with each other, will increase response. For example, sending a letter that is then followed up by a phone call will increase response rate.

Advertising that a canvasser will be visiting your neighborhood soon will increase response.

Personal solicitation: Personal solicitation of someone the solicitor knows: 50 percent response. The solicitor must know that the prospect gives away money and cares about the cause. Because this is the most labor-intensive strategy, it is usually reserved for larger gifts.

The Web: Web sites are a great way to recruit new donors as well as keep existing ones. Every site should have an interactive button on the home page with the words "How You Can Help," or "Join Us." Clicking on this button either brings the user to a form they can download and mail in with a check, or allows them to give on-line using a credit card. If you are not set up to receive gifts on-line, the downloadable form is fine. Other pages of your site describing your work and projects should also have an icon that takes people to where they can give.

Right now most organizations aren't making that much money on their sites; some have concluded the maintenance and effort of a Web site isn't worth it. I think this is a mistake. This new technology is just beginning to be widely accepted and used. We have not begun to realize the potential of the World Wide Web. I would keep at it—it builds on itself.

Extra Gifts from Current Donors

Using any of these strategies, except canvassing, to request extra gifts from current donors will bring 10 percent above the acquisition rate. (Canvassing is not recommended as a strategy for seeking extra gifts unless the project affects the neighborhood where the canvass is occurring.)

In a crisis that is clearly not the fault of your organization, you can get the response rate up to 15 percent. Organizations that work with immigrants, or have been accused of being unpatriotic, or are in big fights with corporations over environmental or health issues will often elicit a lot of sympathy from their donors.

Conversion and Retention

Once a person gives, the organizational goal is to get that person to give again, and then again. At this point, organizations greatly expanding their donor base need to understand the important concept of *conversion rate*.

In fundraising parlance, the conversion rate is the percentage of first-time donors who give a second gift. Many organizations that do well in recruiting new donors are unable to keep them. A healthy conversion rate is around 40 percent. In other words, if you have acquired two hundred first-time donors, you will expect eighty (40 percent) of those people to give a second time.

If you have a lower conversion rate than 40 percent, make sure that your systems for thanking people promptly are in place, your thank-you notes are personalized, you have spelled the donor's name correctly, and you have sent a newsletter, annual report, or some other kind of correspondence between requests for money.

Here's an example. A community theater putting on plays with progressive political themes lost a grant from the National Endowment for the Arts because a play they performed was deemed to be unpatriotic and inappropriately critical of the government. When their next play opened shortly thereafter, they were picketed by an anti-choice group on the grounds that the play had too strong a pro-abortion message. The stress of this time deepened an existing rift between the artistic director and the managing director, who was also the main fundraiser in the presence of a non-fundraising board. The managing director quit with a day's notice. Within two months, the theater was in financial trouble. The Crisis Task Force that formed observed that the public had supported the theater in the face of the controversies in letters to the editor and e-mails to the theater. The team therefore elected to send a large direct mail appeal to a variety of lists of local givers they were able to compile, including donors to the library and civil liberties causes, along with arts patrons. They worked very hard on the mailing, putting personal notes on each letter and following up a number of letters with phone calls. Community outrage at the effort to censor the theater brought in a whopping 12 percent response and $75,000. The financial crisis was fairly easily solved for the moment.

Unfortunately, the group had not made enough of a change in their way of doing fundraising to survive in the long term. The following year, the conversion rate for these donors was only 20 percent, with many of those renewing at a lower level. It was easy to see why. The letter was an impersonal "Dear Friend" and the address was a label, in many cases slightly smeared. Having done so much to get their original donors, they now did nothing special to retain them. Don't make that mistake.

Once donors have given a second time, we speak in terms of *retention rates;* that is, the percentage of donors who give a third year. For donors who give two years in a row, your retention rate for the third year should be about 70 or 80 percent. Your major donor retention rate should be at least 80 percent, giving you an overall retention rate of about 65 percent. In other words, if you have fifteen hundred donors, you will need to acquire five hundred new donors every year. If you have a higher retention rate, it could be because your donor list is too small. If you have a lower retention rate, with more personalization and telephone follow-up on renewal efforts, you can bring your retention rate up to 70 percent or so.

One thing that can temporarily depress your retention rate is having people on your donor list whom we call *crisis donors.* Fires, floods, famine, attacks that are perceived to be bullying or unfair, and the like attract a cross section of big-hearted people who want to help but are not going to make an ongoing commitment to an organization. If your crisis is something very dramatic and well publicized, you will see an influx of these donors. They are a wonderful boost to cash flow, but you need to monitor them so that you do not spend all of their donation trying to get them to give again.

How do you know who these crisis donors are? Obviously, you don't know all of them, but if you have a dramatic event, create a field in your database for unsolicited gifts. Donations that do not come in through a mail appeal (which you can tell because they are not sent in one of your return envelopes) or donations that come in with a note such as, "Mary Smith told me about your fire/theft/police raid. . . . Here's something to help out," should be noted as such. These people are entered into the database and they get a newsletter and other mailings anyone else would get during the year, but when it comes for renewal mailings, send them a special letter referring to their help with the crisis and asking them to become an ongoing supporter. If they do not respond to this letter, remove them from regular mailings. You can keep their names and write to them from to time when you have a dramatic need, which does not have to be a crisis. The same holds true for people who give you memorial gifts. They are memorializing someone for whom your organization was important, but your organization may not be important to them.

Upgrading

The next step in donor development is getting some donors to give more money this year than last. This process is called *upgrading*. All donors are given the opportunity to give more in each mail appeal, but some are identified as prospects for whom a more personal approach would be beneficial. Your upgrade response should be about the same as your personalized acquisition response—in other words, 50 percent of the people you ask to increase their gift should do so if they are properly qualified as prospects and approached personally.

Special Events

Special events can be used for acquisition, retention, and upgrading of donors. They are actually a combination of a number of strategies, so percentage of response is not an evaluation mechanism that is useful for events.

OTHER ANALYSIS

A number of other factors affecting your fundraising success need to be looked at and adjusted if necessary.

Fulfillment Cost

Fulfillment cost is what it costs you to keep a donor. It includes entering the donor's name into your database, the cost of sending a newsletter (paper, printing, postage, staff time), and the cost of renewal mailings. Fulfillment costs should be less than $10 per donor each year. Many organizations have hundreds and sometimes even thousands of people on their mailing lists who are not current donors (that is, they have not made a gift in the last sixteen months) or may never have given at all. Because the fulfillment cost per person is minimal, or more likely the organization never figured out that cost, most organizations leave these non-givers on their lists as a form of outreach. One sometimes hears stories of a person who was kept on an organization's mailing list for five years after giving one gift of $35, then died and left the group $10,000. I am sure this does happen, but keeping hundreds or thousands of people on your list for years in the hope that one will leave you a legacy is not a fundraising strategy. In fact, even if that did happen, the entire value of one bequest could easily have been used up by the cost of keeping all these people on your list all that time. One organization had four thousand people on their mailing list, with nine hundred of them current donors. They figured their fulfillment cost at $3 per person per year, meaning they were spending $9,300 a year on people who were not giving money. That money could be freed up and used for real outreach.

Every year, you need to go through every name and know why these people are on your list. These are the people who should stay on your mailing list:

Donors who have given any amount at least once in the past sixteen months.

Donors who have ever given more than $1,000 at one time. (If they have never given again, they should be approached personally and solicited for another gift, or if they have turned down repeated personal requests, they should be talked with.)

Volunteers who give time but not money.

Current and immediate past funders.

People who have requested to be on the list but cannot pay. They should be told that a request of this kind needs to be made every year.

Vendors, if they request it.

In some cases, politicians, if they are sympathetic to your cause and if they and their staff read your mail.

People who previously were regular givers of any amount but have stopped giving. They too need to be approached personally. After they have not given for two or more years, they need to be removed from the list.

These are the people who do not need to stay on the list and why:

Former board and staff members who do not contribute time or money, unless they specifically request to be on the list. If you're not sure whether a former board or staff member wishes to be kept on the list, ask them. People may have had a great time being on your board ten years ago, but they have gone on. Their interests have changed. If they show no desire to be on the list, take them off. If you want to make sure they don't want to be on the list, call them. Ditto with staff. Many people work for five, ten, or even fifteen or more organizations in their life. They may have loved them all, but they are not people who want to get your newsletter.

Funders who have not given your organization money in three or more years. Funders get a lot of mail; most of it is unread. Newsletters and annual reports are often dutifully placed in their office library or in a file, but funders hardly have time to keep up with the groups they are currently funding or are thinking of funding.

If you are carrying one thousand extra people on your mailing list, you could easily save $2,000 by dropping them and invest that into another fundraising strategy. Maintaining a clean donor list is a great cost saver and allows for real planning.

How Many Donors?

In the corporate world, the analysis of how many customers a business could have is called market penetration. How many customers would ever buy your new product? Who else is trying to sell a similar product? Would they be likely to own two of these products? Organizations whose work is controversial or geographically specific, or who work in rural communities particularly need to look at this issue. Once in a while, I find an organization that has probably attracted all the donors it can and needs to focus on upgrading donors or even moving into earned-income strategies to continue to expand its income. The vast majority of nonprofits, however, are not in that position.

You can hire people to help you figure out your market penetration or you can make a rough guess. Here's how to do the latter.

In the United States and Canada, an average of seven out of ten adults give away money. Some states that have surveyed giving have discovered that their state varies from that average. For example, in Hawaii, 90 percent of adults give money, whereas in Colorado or Alaska, only 60 percent do. Your local community foundation or association of nonprofits may know the percentage of givers for your state or even your county. (See Alliance of Nonprofit Organizations in Resources for how to get a master list of state nonprofit associations.)

If you can't find out, assume seven out of ten people in your community are donors. From this seven, subtract two whose giving is fixed. They have a certain set of charities they give to and are unlikely to add or subtract any. This group includes people who give only to their house of worship. Subtract one more who is a "crisis donor" who may give you money once but will not become an ongoing donor. Subtract one more who only gives to well-established, mainstream organizations and is distrustful or completely unaware of smaller or more grassroots groups.

You are now down to three out of every ten people as possibilities for you. Now think about how well your organization is known in your community. How old is it? How many people do your services or activities reach in a year? If we were to stop people in the street near your office, how likely is it that they would have heard of you? How many other organizations do work similar to yours? How controversial is your organization's work? In answering these questions, be realistic, but also think about how your situation might work in your favor. Being controversial will attract donors as well as repel them. In towns with a large number of arts organizations or environmental groups, these groups find that they can often raise more money than if there were just one or two dealing with their issues. The public has a higher awareness of their issue and sometimes a community's reputation as an arts community or a green community is built from the presence of these nonprofits. Taking all these factors into account will give you a rough sense of what your maximum donor base could be; you can compare that to the number of donors you have now and see how much room there is for growth.

Let's look at two examples. A fifteen-year-old Montessori School in a rural community of five thousand full-time residents has three hundred donors. They have a fairly high attrition rate, as their current donor pool of parents, other relatives, and friends of graduating kids stop giving. A handful of former students are now donors but they are young and it will be a while before there is a critical mass of alumni to raise money from. In figuring out the maximum number of donors they could hope to have, they calculate from the area's population of three thousand adults and assume that twenty-one hundred (70 percent) are donors to any group and 40 percent are already not available to them. This leaves them with 30 percent of the adult population, or a maximum of nine hundred potential donors. The school is well known in the community and well respected, but has always scrambled to raise enough money. It now it finds itself in friendly competition with the public elementary and high schools, which have recently had to slash their art and music programs and have embarked on their own fundraising programs. With this competition of the public schools, the Montessori School starts raising less money than they have in years past. In looking at their situation, they realize that 10 percent of the donors in the community already give to the school; it seems unlikely that more will do so. To avoid a funding crisis, they need to create another income stream to augment the income from donors.

This information keeps the Montessori School from spending a lot of effort trying to widen their donor base. Instead, they focus on creative uses of their school. The town does not have a community center and the Montessori School has a fairly large cafeteria and gymnasium complex, with moveable walls, lots of tables and chairs, and a playground and grassy area outside. They offer this space as a community center in evenings and week-ends and take in money from the a rental fees. This earned-income strategy begins to help them meet their budget and has the potential for growth.

A second example comes from a group we'll call Alliance Against Poisoned Rivers (AAPR). It is organizing in communities downstream from a paper mill that has been polluting the local river for many years. Since the mill is a major employer, demands to improve its practices have simply caused it to threaten to move overseas. Water tests show that some toxins are leaching into the communities' well water. The smell from the stream wafts over the community nearest the mill; fish and wildlife have suffered.

AAPR has four hundred people on its mailing list, many of whom are donors. About one hundred of the donors are from out of state. The group's records are not very accurate, as they have been primarily supported by foundations and have done very little fundraising to generate individual donations. Now, one of their main funders, a family foundation, has gone out of business. Other funders have notified the organization that they, too, will no longer be funding them. In another setback, the group has been unable to replace the founding executive director, who recently left. The board is made up of activists and scientists, none of whom are interested in fundraising. The scientists suggest writing more proposals and the activists suggest cutting staff. Everyone is convinced that the group is too controversial to be able to raise money from a broad base of individuals.

However, there is reason to believe that they are wrong. More than thirty thousand adults in four communities downstream from the mill can smell the mill's pollution. In addition, there are two environmentally conscious communities with a total of about five thousand adults upstream from the mill. A donor with a background in direct mail offers to bankroll a mass mailing to these communities. He thinks the group should be able to build a donor base of twenty-five hundred people over a couple of years. This would be about 6 percent of the adult population, far fewer, in his reasoning, than those who are adversely affected by the mill.

Using a reverse directory, AAPR is able to get the name and address of every household in the six communities. They tailor each letter and envelope to the community, even putting a small map on the front of the letter showing where the town is in relation to the mill. The mailing receives a 2 percent response, remarkable because it was sent to all households, 30 percent of which do not donate. With 700 new donors and $31,000 from just one mailing, the organization realizes that they have far more support than they have ever mobilized.

This organization is saved from a more serious crisis by the donor who bankrolls the mailing, not so much because of the money raised, although that is certainly helpful, but because they are given a clear sense of their potential for building a donor base at no cost to themselves. This donor helped them focus on raising money rather than cutting programs, which was what the board might have been inclined to do. AAPR is not out of danger yet, but the momentum they have generated and the morale boost they are feeling will carry them through.

Time Spent for Money Raised

Another aspect of analysis is to look at how much time is spent on each strategy in your fundraising plan in relation to how much money it brings in. Could this time be better spent on another strategy? Are you getting enough other valuable outcomes (publicity, new donors, visibility) to make the time worth it? Is this a longer-term strategy from which you wouldn't expect a lot of money just yet, such as planned giving?

When you do this analysis, you may notice that during the crisis, people close to the group were willing to suspend their discomfort with asking for money and actually raise money through solicitation. Now that the crisis has abated, they are back to being uncomfortable and are suggesting strategies that don't require much personal solicitation on their part: celebrity golf tournaments run by specialists in large special events, more proposal writing ("There must be some foundations we haven't approached"), and the all-purpose suggestion, "Cut overhead." Showing people how much money the organization is able to raise using various strategies will help board and staff stay on track. It will also ensure that you don't spend time on strategies that, for whatever reason, are not working for your group.

There are three other areas to analyze with regard to how time is spent: your fundraising team, foundations, and meetings.

Your Fundraising Team. Anyone in fundraising knows that follow-up is key. A board member says he will call five people, but he doesn't unless someone else reminds him, and probably reminds him more than once. But how often does this have to occur for the work to get done? This analysis is very important. If it takes a staff person two hours in phone calls and e-mails to a board member who actually makes five calls, which take her two hours and bring in two gifts of $1,000, it has taken four hours to earn $2,000, at a rate of $500 in for each hour spent. This is clearly worth it. If the two donors give $100 each, then the group has earned $50 an hour, which is not worth it. However, if a staff person has to spend only thirty minutes in follow-up and the board member spends one hour calling for two gifts of $100, then the average is $133 an hour. If, after two hours of reminder calls and e-mails, the board member never does anything and the staff person winds up making the calls herself, it almost doesn't matter what the donors give because the whole idea of being a team has been undermined.

Without driving yourself crazy, try to keep track of the time things take. At the end of any campaign, look at the time put in for what you got out of it. See if there are ways you could use less time next time—often just knowing what to do saves time. What do you wish you had known ahead of time? Make sure you tell the next campaign chair that information. And do your best not to work with volunteers who waste your time.

Foundations. A recent study showed that an organization spends, on average, one hundred hours on every grant proposal. This includes time spent finding the foundation, contacting them, writing the proposal, and writing the required reports. Depending on how well you pay your staff, this is an investment of $2,000 to $3,000. There is little point in applying for less than $10,000, since for the same money you could invest in a special event, a mail appeal, or a major gifts campaign and make the same or more money year after year.

Meetings. During a crisis, people love to meet. A meeting is a place to process feelings and vent frustration. Meetings can be comforting and even fun. At the end of a meeting, you feel as though you have done work whether you have or not. Certainly, meetings are a critical feature of getting through a crisis, but be sure you don't get in the habit of meeting just for the sake of it, or because the group is procrastinating doing its fundraising. Every meeting should have a purpose, an agenda, minutes, and a brief evaluation. If you track the person-power going into meetings, you will be sure to use them wisely. Twelve people in a three-hour meeting have just spent the equivalent of a week of work (thirty-six hours). Ask yourself if that time, which you will never see again, has significantly helped pull your organization through this crisis.

We all have the same amount of time—twenty-four hours in our day—and when a day is over, we cannot get that time back. We have to use our time wisely; to do that requires paying attention to how we use it and how we could use it better.

When to Spend Money

There are times during your crisis when spending money is exactly the right thing to do. Here are just a few examples:

Have food and drinks available at meetings. It doesn't have to be a lot and it doesn't have to be fancy, but people will appreciate the refreshment and do better work.

Send volunteers and staff to daylong training sessions to help them acquire or improve skills they need in order to get through this time. The sessions don't have to be expensive or far away, but high-functioning teams train and practice. They know they can always improve their skills.

Don't tolerate inadequate equipment—computers, software, copy machines. You don't need to have the most modern and the most deluxe, but your machines need to work easily and smoothly. You do not need to use up time dealing with bad equipment that should be helping you raise money.

SUMMARY

By paying close attention to what is working and how to make it work better, what isn't working and how to fix it or let it go, who is working and how to help them work better and feel good about their work, you begin to see how to create a new fundraising plan. It takes time to do all that I am suggesting, but it takes far more time not to do it. I am greatly helped by the Buddhist saying, "We have so little time, we must proceed very slowly."

CHAPTER 10

Conquering Tomorrow's Crises Today

Someone asked me in a workshop recently, "What is the future for non-profits if the economy continues to be bad? After all, there is no guar-antee that we will come out of this downward cycle any time soon." I had to tell him that his statement is correct. In fact, even if the all aspects of the economy recover rather quickly (unlikely), it will take the sector two or three years to catch up. For example, foundation giving will not begin to go up again until there are three good years in the five-year average, as ex-plained in the Introduction. As people become employed again, they may still have debts they incurred during their unemployment and will not re-sume giving at their former levels immediately. An improved economy will not automatically trigger a resumption of government funding to non-profits, since that kind of funding is driven not only by economics but also by government priorities. It will take years to recover from this "perfect storm," and in fact, because the world is changing so quickly and problems can appear very quickly, nonprofit organizations probably need to learn to live in a state of endemic uncertainty.

As for answering the trainee's question, of course I don't pretend to know what the future actually holds in terms of external factors such as the economy, but I do know what the future needs to be for each organization and for the nonprofit sector as a whole if nonprofits are to have the impact they should and if they are to function at maximum health and effective-ness. That is the subject of this chapter.

THE MOST IMPORTANT CHANGE

About once a year for the past twenty years, I have had the following experience: I have several trips coming up and for each I have a long to-do list of details that must be handled before I leave; I also have three or four writing deadlines. That's when my car decides to break down and one of my cats has to be rushed to the vet and then given medicine four times a day. Though I may not be at my most calm, I am able to do it all. I keep my lists in front of me; I make my plan and work my plan. Most of the time I am thinking, "When this is over (the travel or writing or a personal crisis), I have a couple weeks of nothing. That will be great. That's when I'll catch up on my e-mail, go to the library, and have dinner with friends." Then the day comes—the day before my easy two weeks. I feel really tired and go to bed early. I wake up the next morning with a terrible cold or flu. I finally have time to be sick!

The same is true with organizations. A crisis happens—they figure it out, they hold it together for the weeks or sometimes months that are required. Finally, one day, the Crisis Task Force meets and decides they can disband. Things are back on track—at least as much as they can be. Within a few days, staff are ill and several board members request leaves of absence. The computer hard drives crash completely and the toilet backs up, spewing contaminated water on the cheap wall-to-wall carpeting. After a while, everyone recovers and comes back to work, the plumbing is repaired and a new carpet installed. Everyone sits and looks at each other and thinks, "Now what?"

It is not possible to maintain the level of excitement and attention that a crisis inspires, nor is it healthy; fortunately, it is also unnecessary.

What we want after a crisis is the kind of energy and enthusiasm people have who like—and believe in—their work. They like it every day, and every morning when they get up and get ready for work they are happy to be going. They are happy because they feel they are making a difference or making a contribution to the community, not just making a salary. But they also look forward to the weekend and to their vacations. Work is important and meaningful, but it is not everything.

Board members need to look forward to meetings the way they look forward to a discussion with a group of interesting, informed people with a diversity of viewpoints. Their meetings need to be interesting as well as challenging, and it should be satisfying to catch up on what's been happening and make plans for how their organization should grow and change, or how they can improve their functioning, or whatever is most important at that moment. When this is the case, board members do their work outside of meetings willingly, but they do not take on more than their share.

An important outcome of the crisis must be that the organization uses the interruption in their "normal" way of working to analyze how they work normally and to make course corrections in that way of functioning. There is no point in going back to working the way you did, which contributed to the crisis in the first place.

So, in this post-crisis environment, be very vigilant that your new work habits and your productive team efforts continue. Create and keep fostering a different organizational culture than the one that allowed you to be so vulnerable to the "perfect storm" that is still engulfing so many nonprofits.

OTHER ORGANIZATIONAL CHANGES

Demands for accountability of the nonprofit sector will continue to rise. Scandals in both the for-profit and nonprofit sectors that now seem to be revealed weekly are causing the public a great deal of concern. In order to regain the public trust, nonprofits need to be squeaky clean and figure out all the ways they can show how well they steward money and what they use it for. Financial statements posted on Web sites and board members' thorough reviews of expenses and income annually, as well as during the budget process and through regular financial reporting, must become de rigueur. But nonprofits must also educate the public on what to look for in a nonprofit organization. Simply spending money wisely is not a guarantee of effective programs, and mismanagement of funds does not always mean the organization did not do good work. Use your annual report, annual general meeting, Web site, and newsletter to discuss your work and how it is paid for. Talk about how much it costs and how much more it would cost if you didn't have volunteers. Talk about the role and legitimate costs of administration. Be as transparent as you possibly can.

Being appointed or elected to a board of directors must be seen both as more prestigious and also more serious than it has in the past. Organizations should not ask someone to be on a board casually, and people should not take on board responsibilities lightly. Moreover, much more work needs to be done by a constantly shifting cadre of volunteers who are willing to work but don't want full board responsibility. Then, board members will be able to focus on their work, knowing that they need to do their job, but that their job is not to do all the work that the staff or volunteers can't do. Board and staff must work more in partnership and not see each other as adversaries or roadblocks.

CHANGES IN THE SECTOR AS A WHOLE

The nonprofit sector must become better organized and wield more influence over regulation of their functioning. A congressperson would never look outside their office today and think, "Oh, no, the nonprofit lobby is here. I'd better pay attention to them." Professional associations of nonprofits, think tanks, and public policy institutes dealing with the sector itself are beginning to pull organizations together to present a united front on issues of legislation and regulation regarding nonprofits. Developing these positions must continue to happen even more systematically. To be sure, the sector will not always be united in what it wants, what it thinks the government should do, what regulations should be in place, and so on, but sectorwide discussion is needed on all these issues. When we can achieve unity on an issue, we need to use our power to influence decision makers in their policy making and the press in how they report about us.

People are beginning to see the fundamental work that nonprofits do in every community. As funding for social services, arts, and schools continues to be cut, everyone will feel the burden and must be encouraged to ask questions about the fairness of these cuts. As the sector becomes more organized and these questions become more focused, people will begin to demand that their taxes be used to meet at least basic needs; that public schools, public parks, public libraries, public pools, and so on actually be funded by the public and be open to the public. This change is already happening in many communities and needs to become a national movement. Fundraising will be key to a lot of this protest, as members of the public begin to question the need for private fundraising efforts for public services and focus their fundraising efforts on organizing strategies instead. In other words, rather than passively trying to replace government funding with private funding, communities and organizations must raise money to advocate with government at the local, state, and even federal levels about what taxes should be used for and for a more just and equitable tax system.

Professionalism in the nonprofit sector will have to be redefined. During the 1990s, volunteer or activist activities were replaced with paid staff positions. This was often a good thing, as staff could do many jobs more efficiently and consistently and volunteers were freed to do other work. However, in many organizations, paid professionals inadvertently drove out volunteers. Organizations became staff-driven and boards became rubber stamps for executive director initiatives. Decisions about program direction were conceived, discussed, and decided by staff and then reported to the board. Involvement of the larger community became negligible. In the worst cases, volunteers, community members, or board members who attempted to influence program direction were met with resistance and sometimes hostility. The implicit response was, "We are professionals. We know best." In the future, a different partnership between staff, board, and outside community members will have to be forged. The characteristics of this partnership will vary according to the size and type of group, but involvement of all parties in program direction will be a sign of efficiency rather than a roadblock to getting the work done. Professionalism will still be important— we cannot return to the full-time volunteer model because few people can afford to be full-time volunteers anymore. But a more democratic and inclusive model of decision making will characterize successful organizations. Again, fundraising will be key to this involvement. Inviting everyone to be a donor at whatever level works for them, along with building relationships with donors, will automatically mean more input from a broader community.

CHANGES IN FUNDRAISING

In addition to changes in the sector as a whole, fundraising must change in some fundamental ways if we are to be able to raise the money we need and attract good people to the profession.

Fundraising and program work must be integrated so that development directors are seen as coordinators of fundraising efforts. Those efforts must be undertaken not only by the development directors but also by other staff people, board members, and volunteers. Program staff and organizers must understand fundraising and be able to take advantage of opportunities they have to raise money, and development people must be included in program planning.

Technology needs to play an ever more important role in fundraising: Web sites, e-newsletters, listservs, on-line bulletin boards, and the like will all be part of program and fundraising efforts. More and more people will give on-line and be involved in the organization virtually. Having and fully using a full-functioning database will be the key to the donor analysis I have talked about in this book. Having people on staff and among volunteers who are tech savvy will be imperative.

Organizations need to seek out new types of donors—people who have historically been overlooked in the search for donors but who will make up a larger and larger part of the population in the future—people between the ages of eighteen and twenty-five, immigrants, poor people, and people who grew up poor but are no longer poor. Having people on staff who speak and can write languages other than English will be important and in states like California imperative. Understanding different cultural forms of giving will be critical, and making sure your programs are culturally appropriate will be the key to success.

In addition to new donors, the large aging population of baby boomers need to be dealt with differently than younger people. Generational differences will become more pronounced as people live longer and organizations deal with a multicultural mix spanning three or four generations.

WHAT WILL NEVER CHANGE

There are three things about fundraising that have never and will never change:

1. People give when they are asked.

2. Once they give, they must be thanked.

3. Once they are thanked, they are ready to be asked again for more or for help in another way—with their time, advice, contacts, and so forth.

Fundraising is all about building relationships—inviting people to join an organization and continuing to invite them to be part of it. Remember that seven out of ten people give away money. They can give it to your group or to another group, but it will be given away. Your job is to get on their menu of choices.

To maintain a donor base and attract new donors every year, an organization must remain mission-driven. To remain mission-driven requires a larger team involved in fundraising than just a few board or staff members.

In this book I have tried to make three points:

1. This is a weird and difficult time to raise money; many organizations are not going to survive this time.

2. Your organization can survive—in fact it can grow. Use this time to make the changes you need to make. Then not only will you get through this crisis, you won't be vulnerable to other crises.

3. You can survive and grow if you don't sacrifice what you stand for.

There are organizations that do good work that will not survive this next period. Sadly, some of them have already gone out of business. There are other organizations that do not do good work that will survive. They will be able to raise money and continue to fool people into thinking their work has some value. But good groups that survive and grow will be in the leadership of the sector and produce the kind of leaders the country so desperately needs.

Over time, the future will hold for us a country and a world where people are more important than profit and where what is good for the whole of creation is the driving force of all that is done in the corporate, governmental, and nonprofit sectors.

REFERENCES

American Association of Fund Raising Counsel Trust for Philanthropy. *Giving USA Update,* no. 4. Indianapolis: American Association of Fund Raising Counsel, 2002.

American Association of Fund Raising Counsel Trust for Philanthropy. "Charity Holds Its Own in Tough Times." American Association of Fund Raising Counsel Press Release, June 23, 2003. http://aafrc.org/press_releases/trustreleases/charityholds.html.

American Civil Liberties Union. "Threats to Civil Liberties Post-September 11: Secrecy, Erosion of Privacy, Danger of Unchecked Government." Statement by Gregory T. Nojeim, American Civil Liberties Union News Release, Dec. 14, 2001. www.aclu.org/news/2001/n121401b.html.

"Current State of Philanthropy in America." *News Hour.* OnLine Forum. Public Broadcasting System, Jan. 1, 1998. http://www.pbs.org/newshour/forum/january98/philanthropy_1-1.html.

Gary, T., and Kohner, M. (rev. ed.) *Inspired Philanthropy.* San Francisco: Jossey-Bass, 2002.

Collins, C., and others. *Robin Hood Was Right.* New York: Norton, 2000.

Henderson, J. "Groups vs. Teams." *Grassroots Fundraising Journal,* July/Aug. 2002, *21*(4), 10.

INDEPENDENT SECTOR. "Giving and Volunteering in the United States," 2001, pp. 28–29.

Klein, K. *Fundraising for the Long Haul.* San Francisco: Jossey-Bass, 2000.

Klein, K. "Why Good Fundraisers Are Never Paid on Commission." In K. Klein and S. Roth (eds.), *Raise More Money: The Best of the Grassroots Fundraising Journal.* San Francisco: Jossey-Bass, 2001.

Lichtblau, E. "Charity Leader Accepts a Deal in a Terror Case." *New York Times,* Feb. 11, 2003.

Mogil, C., and Slepian, A. *We Gave Away a Fortune.* Philadelphia: New Society, 1993.

Moyers, B. "Bill Moyers Interviews Chuck Lewis," *NOW with Bill Moyers.* Public Affairs Television, February 7, 2003. http://www.pbs.org/now/transcript/transcript_lewis2.htm.

Moyers, R. L. "A Shocking Silence on Muslim Charities." *Chronicle of Philanthropy,* Oct. 17, 2002.

OMB Watch. "Anti-Terrorism Bill Could Impact Nonprofits." *Watcher,* Nov. 14, 2001. http://www.ombwatch.org/article/articleview/288/1/41/.

Salamon, L. *The State of Nonprofit America.* Washington, D.C.: Brookings Institution, 2002.

Williamson, R. "Islamic Charities Pursue Mission in Dramatically Altered United States." *NonProfit Times,* Sept. 1, 2002.

RESOURCES

This section contains books, magazines, and Web sites I have found most helpful for effective fundraising, along with a complete list of books and materials I have developed.

One of the most valuable ways to find out more about fundraising is to visit the Foundation Center Collection nearest you. The Foundation Center, headquartered in New York City, is a nonprofit library service supported by foundations, fees for service, products for sale, and other fundraising strategies. The Center collects and disseminates information about foundations, corporations, government, and all other types of fundraising and proposal writing. A list of Foundation Centers and their cooperating collections (that is, public libraries or other locations that have materials from the Foundation Center) can be found on-line at www.fdncenter.org.

Note that the resources in the section on Web sites are not specifically about fundraising or philanthropy, but they can help with the many other questions common to nonprofit organizations.

The titles in the following section can be ordered on-line at www.josseybass. org/gochardon.

OTHER TITLES IN THE JOSSEY-BASS CHARDON PRESS SERIES

Gary, T., and Kohner, M. (rev. ed.) *Inspired Philanthropy.* San Francisco: Jossey-Bass, 2002.
A step-by-step workbook on how to match your giving with your values.

Klein, K. *Ask and You Shall Receive: A Fundraising Training Program for Religious Organizations and Projects.* San Francisco: Jossey-Bass, 1999.
  In two parts: Leader Manual and Participant Manual.
Klein, K. *Fundraising for the Long Haul.* San Francisco: Jossey-Bass, 2000.
  For older social-change organizations exploring their particular challenges. Case studies, personal experience, and how-to instructions.
Robinson, A. *Selling Social Change (Without Selling Out): Earned Income Strategies for Nonprofits.* San Francisco: Jossey-Bass, 2001.
  Shows how organizations committed to social justice can build responsible and profitable businesses. Dozens of examples along with what to watch out for in pursuing earned income.
Robinson, E. *The Membership Tool Kit.* San Francisco: Jossey-Bass, 2003.
  Excellent step-by-step guide to building a membership organization by one of the leaders in the field.
Sen, R. *Stir It Up: Lessons in Community Organizing and Advocacy.* San Francisco: Jossey-Bass, 2003.
  The steps of building and mobilizing a constituency and implementing key strategies for social change.

OTHER FUNDRAISING MATERIALS FROM KIM KLEIN

Order the publications in this section from *Grassroots Fundraising Journal,* 3781 Broadway, Oakland, Calif. 94611, 888-458-8588, or www.grassroots-fundraising.org.

Grassroots Fundraising Journal.
  Bimonthly how-to periodical.
"Information Systems for Fundraising." *Grassroots Fundraising Journal,* May/June 2002 (entire issue), *21*(3).
  Contains information on fundraising databases.
Klein, K., and Roth, S. *The Board of Directors.* (3rd ed.) Oakland, Calif.: Grassroots Fundraising Journal, 1999.
  Ten articles on creating and building an effective board of directors reprinted from the *Grassroots Fundraising Journal.*
Klein, K. *Getting Major Gifts.* (rev. ed.) Oakland, Calif.: *Grassroots Fundraising Journal,* 1999.
  Twelve articles on developing major gifts reprinted from the *Grassroots Fundraising Journal.*

MORE USEFUL FUNDRAISING MATERIALS

American Association of Fund Raising Counsel Trust for Philanthropy. *Giving USA: Annual Report on Philanthropy.* Indianapolis: American Association of Fund Raising Counsel.

Analysis of giving and trends in philanthropy.

Flanagan, J. *The Grassroots Fundraising Book.* Chicago: Contemporary Books, 1992.

Excellent introductory book for small organizations.

Flanagan, J. *Successful Fundraising: A Complete Handbook for Volunteers and Professionals.* Chicago: Contemporary Books, 1991.

How-to book on large-scale fundraising events and campaigns.

"Grassroots Fundraising: The Kim Klein Video Series."

Seven topics are covered in twenty-minute sessions in a professionally produced video series with accompanying workbook. Order from Grassroots Institute for Fundraising Training (GIFT), www.grassrootsinstitute.org.

Rosso, H. (ed.). *Achieving Excellence in Fundraising.* (rev. ed.) San Francisco: Jossey-Bass, 2003.

The late Henry Rosso was one of the most famous fundraising consultants in America. This introduction to the theory and practice of fundraising is an invaluable tool.

Stallings, B., and McMillion, D. *How to Produce Fabulous Fundraising Events: Reap Remarkable Returns with Minimal Effort.* Pleasanton, Calif.: Building Better Skills (1717 Courtney Ave., Suite 201, Pleasanton, Calif. 94588, 925-426-8335).

The title says it all.

Wendroff, A. *Special Events: Proven Strategies for Nonprofit Fundraising.* New York: Wiley, 2002.

A masterly guide to producing large special events.

OTHER PERIODICALS

Chronicle of Philanthropy. Order from Chronicle of Philanthropy, 1255 23rd St. NW, Washington, D.C. 20037.

Biweekly publication.

NonProfit Quarterly. Order from www.nonprofitquarterly.org or Third Sector New England, 18 Tremont Street, #700, Boston, Mass. 02108, 800-281-7770.

Each issue focuses on a theme of importance to the sector. Sample articles are on the Web site.

WEB SITES

Accountants for the Public Interest (API), www.accountingnet.com/asso/api/index.html.

Questions and answers as well as materials on accounting for nonprofits.

Alliance for Nonprofit Management, www.genie.org.

"Nonprofit Genie" provides answers to frequently asked management questions.

Alliance of Nonprofit Organizations, www.alliance.org-check.

Provides a master list of state nonprofit associations showing what percentage of people in a state are givers.

Building Movement Project, www.buildingmovement.org.

Helpful information on the nonprofit sector as a whole, particularly new laws and regulations and analysis for organizations working for social justice. Check out the column "Jack's Corner," written by Kim's cat.

CompassPoint, www.compasspoint.org.

Training, consulting, and research on nonprofit management, concepts, and strategies.

Internet Nonprofit Center, www.nonprofit-info.org/npofaq.

Information, advice, and articles on numerous nonprofit management topics, including information on how to calculate program costs or fundraising ratios, or how to value donated goods.

Professional Support Software, www.FundraiserSoftware.com.

Excellent database software for small nonprofits; samples can be downloaded.

Technical Assistance for Community Organizations (TACS), www.tacs.org.

Good place to shop for accounting software.

United for a Fair Economy, www.ufenet.org.

Works toward closing the gap between rich and poor with clear information about economics, taxes, and the relationship of the distribution of money to the quality of life of most Americans. Web site and newsletter are accessible and useful.

INDEX

of, 1–2; organizational patterns leading to, 34; permanent change after, 156–157; size of nonprofit sector as factor in, 7–10; war on terrorism as factor in, 5–7

Crisis donors, 143–144

Crisis Task Force, 35–49; dissolution of, 100; establishment of, 35–37; financial need determined by, 46–47, 88; information gathering by, 38–49, 54; long-term involvement of members of, 118; meetings of, 37, 39–41; reports on decisions of, 48–49; tasks of, 37–38

Current donors: bequests from, 132–133; best practices for working with, 121–133; database of, 122–124; mail appeals to, 106–107; ongoing communication with, 131–132; phone-a-thons to, 103–105; requesting extra gifts from, 141; retention of, 75–76, 131–132, 142–144; segmenting, 122–131; upgrading, 76–77, 144. *See also* Donors

D

Damage control, as message, 55–56

Database: annual review of, 145–146; of individual donors, 122–124

Development staff: job responsibilities of, 15–16; responsibility vs. authority of, 24–25; short campaigns as advantage for, 73. *See also* Staff

Dinner dances, 110–112

Diversity: in funding sources, 70–72, 80, 136; of people involved in fundraising, 72

Domini, A., 17

Donor relations: disorganized approach to, 18; gracious reception of gifts as, 97. *See also* Follow-up

Donors: acquisition of, 75, 139–141; and administrative costs, 21–23; and anti-terrorism measures, 6–7; crisis, 143–144; enlisting in short-term fundraising strategy, 88–97; information on crisis given to, 48, 54–68; in "inner circle" of prospects, 90–91; major, 62, 63–66, 76–77, 144; new types of, in future,

160–161; potential, calculating number of, 146–150; reasons cited by, for not giving, 51–52; recognition for giving by, 74, 76–77; reluctance to ask for money from, 16–18, 85; wealthy, 4, 14. *See also* Current donors; Individual donors

E

E-mail: caution on delivering message via, 62–63; for follow-up on appeal letter, 95; for newsletters, 131–132, 140

Earned income: examples of development of stream of, 83–84, 134–135, 148–149; help with strategy for, 120; as source of income for nonprofits, 14, 71, 72, 133–134

Economic downturn: effect on funding sources, 3–5, 71; effect on nonprofits, 2–5; reasons cited by donors for not giving during, 51–52

Education of public, by nonprofit sector, 20–21, 157–158

Employees. *See* Staff

Endowments: economic downturn's effect on, 3; as funding source during crisis, 42, 44–46

Equipment, spending money on, 152

Escape plan, in message to major donors, 65–66

Estate taxes, 20

Executive director: dealing with death of, 59–61; financial scandals created by behavior of, 66–67; interim, 47–48

External crises, 1–2

F

Facts, known by Crisis Task Force members, 39–41

Faith, 11

Financial needs: immediate, 46–47; for next three months, 88

Financial reserves: example of use of, 45–46; as funding source during crisis, 42, 44–46

Flexibility, in fundraising plans, 72–73, 80

Follow-up: on fundraising activities, 112; with prospects, 94–96

Foundation Center, 165

Foundations: analysis of time spent on vs. money obtained from, 151; crisis due to loss of funding from, 27–28, 31–32; and economic downturn, 3, 71; as source of income for nonprofits, 14, 71, 115–116, 138

Freedom of Information Act (FOIA), 7

Fulfillment cost, 144–146

Funders: information on crisis given to, 48; message delivery by, 56, 62. *See also* Foundations, Corporations, Government

Funding of nonprofits: cutting costs to solve problems with, 24, 41; economic downturn's effect on, 2–5, 71; response to problems with, 24–25; sources of, 13–14, 70–72, 138. *See also specific sources of funding*

Fundraising: case statement's importance in, 52–54; costs of, 23; and financial reserves, 45; functions of, 75; future of, 160–162; high-touch, 73–77, 81–82, 122; incorporating uncertainty in, 69–73; integrating organizational program with, 34; long-term perspective in, 115; as problem vs. symptom of problem, 27; scaled-back, 100–101; to solve funding problems, 24–25; as team effort, 77. *See also* Analysis of fundraising program; Fundraising by organizations in crisis

Fundraising activities: choosing, 113–114; descriptions of, 102–112; evaluating, 101–102; events offering combination of, 144; follow-up on, 112; improvising variations of, 112–113

Fundraising by organizations in crisis, 85–97; asking for money in, 85–87; examples of successful, 78, 80–84; follow-up in, 94–96; gift-range chart for, 88; gracious reception of gifts in, 97; identifying "inner circle" of prospects for, 88–91; mail appeals in, 91–94; team for, 77, 96; timing of, 73, 96

Fundraising plan: Crisis Task Force's review of, 42; flexibility in, 72–73; in message to major donors, 64

Fundraising strategies: long-term, 115–136; for organizations in crisis, 88–97; for period after crisis resolution, 99–114; reason for choosing, 74–75

Future: of fundraising, 160–162; of non-profit sector, 155–160

G

Garage sales, 102–103

Gary, T., 16

Gates, B., Sr., 20

Gift-range chart, 88

Goodwill Industries, scandal in, 8

Government: anti-terrorism provisions of, 5–7; and economic downturn, 5, 71; loss of funding from, 29–30, 57–59; and public debate over taxes, 19–21, 159; as source of income for nonprofits, 14, 71, 138

Groups, vs. teams, 77–78, 79–80

H

Harrington, J., 17

Health insurance, 24

Henderson, J., 77–78, 79–80

High-touch fundraising, 73–77, 81–82, 122

House parties, 108–109

I

Immediate financial need, Crisis Task Force's determination of, 46–47

Immediate needs, Crisis Task Force's determination of, 47–48

Immigrants: effect of war on terrorism on work with, 5; verifying status of, as problem, 29–30

INDEPENDENT SECTOR, 14

Individual donors: advantage of broad base of, 115–116; building base of, 116–121; and economic downturn, 3–4; household participation in giving by, 9; recognition for, 74, 76–77; as

THE AUTHOR

Kim Klein is widely regarded as one of the most important figures in the field of grassroots fundraising, both as a writer and a practitioner. She is best known for adapting traditional fundraising techniques, particularly major donor campaigns, to the needs of smaller organizations—those with budgets of less than $1 million—working for social justice.

Klein began her fundraising career while studying to be a Methodist minister and working in a shelter for battered women in San Francisco. Since then, she has been development director, board member, and volunteer for numerous organizations working for social change.

Klein is the editor of the Chardon Press Series of Jossey-Bass Publishers and the founder and publisher of the bimonthly *Grassroots Fundraising Journal*, which just celebrated twenty-two years of continuous publication. She is also the author of *Fundraising for Social Change* (now in its fourth edition), *Fundraising for the Long Haul*, and *Ask and You Shall Receive: A Fundraising Training Program for Religious Organizations and Projects*. Her most recent book is the anthology *Raise More Money: The Best of the Grassroots Fundraising Journal*, coedited with Stephanie Roth. She has also made a popular video series on fundraising, distributed by the Grassroots Institute for Fundraising Training in Denver.

Widely in demand as a speaker, Klein has provided training and consultation in all fifty states and in eighteen countries. In 1998, she was named Outstanding Fund Raising Executive of the Year by the Golden Gate Chapter of the National Society of Fund Raising Executives. She can be contacted at kimklein@grassrootsfundraising.org.

RESOURCES FOR SOCIAL CHANGE
AVAILABLE FROM JOSSEY-BASS AND CHARDON PRESS

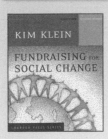

Fundraising for Social Change
FOURTH EDITION
Kim Klein

Thoroughly updated and expanded, this long-awaited fourth edition of *Fundraising for Social Change* offers hands-on, accessible fundraising techniques geared to nonprofits with budgets of less than $1 million that want to raise money from their biggest source of donations—individuals. This widely used guide features expanded chapters on how to ask for money and plan major gifts campaigns, plus new chapters on Internet fundraising and on how to work effectively with your executive director.

"*Fundraising for Social Change* is a must for anyone involved in fundraising—from the smallest community-based group to regional and national organizations. Kim Klein makes the art of fundraising user-friendly. In more than thirty years of fundraising and grant making for progressive efforts, I have not found a more worthwhile tool."

—Ray Santiago, Seva Foundation

Paperback ISBN: 0-7879-6174-4

Fundraising for the Long Haul
Kim Klein

In this companion to her classic, *Fundraising for Social Change*, Kim Klein distills her twenty-five years of experience and wisdom to provide the practical guidance for sustaining a long-term commitment to social change for organizations that are understaffed and under-resourced.

Paperback ISBN: 0-7879-6173-6

Raise More Money:
The Best of the Grassroots Fundraising Journal
Kim Klein, Stephanie Roth, Editors

"When I want to know the answer to a fundraising question, or a way to motivate and teach others, I go to some of the best fundraisers in the business—whose writing appears in this amazing collection of articles from the *Grassroots Fundraising Journal*."

—Joan Garner, Southern Partners Fund

Whether you are a new or seasoned fundraiser, this collection of the best articles from the *Grassroots Fundraising Journal* will provide you with new inspiration to help bring in more money for your organization. Filled with strategies and guidance, this unprecedented anthology shows you how small nonprofits can raise money from their communities and develop long-term financial stability.

Paperback ISBN: 0-7879-6175-2

Ask and You Shall Receive:
A Fundraising Training Program for Religious Organizations and Projects
Kim Klein

The *Ask and You Shall Receive* training package is a do-it-yourself, start-to-finish program on jump-starting fundraising efforts. Realistic time allowances keep the training within reach of busy volunteers.

Paperback ISBN: 0-7879-5563-9

(Includes 1 Leader's Guide and 1 Workbook)

Stir It Up:
Lessons in Community Organizing and Advocacy

Rinku Sen

Sponsored by the Ms. Foundation for Women

If social change organizations local, regional, and national are to succeed, they must go beyond traditional grassroots organizing efforts and develop systematic, comprehensive organizing practices that will change public policy and practice.

Stir It Up, written by renowned activist and trainer Rinku Sen, identifies the key priorities and strategies that can help advance the mission of any social change group. This groundbreaking book addresses the unique challenges and opportunities the new global economy poses for activist groups and provides concrete guidance for community organizations of all orientations.

Paperback   ISBN: 0-7879-6533-2

Roots of Justice:
Stories of Organizing in Communities of Color

Larry R. Salomon

Recaptures some of the nearly forgotten histories of communities of color. These are the stories of people who fought back against exploitation and injustice—and won. *Roots of Justice* shows how ordinary people have made extraordinary contributions to change society.

Paperback   ISBN: 0-7879-6178-7

Making Policy, Making Change
How Communities Are Taking Law into Their Own Hands

Makani N. Themba

"A much-needed life jacket for those committed to progressive social change. In a straightforward, full-blast recitation from one who knows, Makani Themba weaves powerful stories of grassroots struggles to shape and construct policy. This book is a requiem for apathy and inaction."

—*Clarence Lusane, assistant professor, School of International Service, American University*

Paperback   ISBN: 0-7879-6179-5

Selling Social Change (Without Selling Out):
Earned Income Strategies for Nonprofits

Andy Robinson

In *Selling Social Change (Without Selling Out)* expert fundraising trainer and consultant Andy Robinson shows nonprofit professionals how to initiate and sustain successful earned income ventures that provide financial security and advance an organization's mission. Step by step, this invaluable resource shows how to organize a team, select a venture, draft a business plan, find start-up funding, and successfully market goods and services. Robinson includes critical information on the tax implications of earned income and the pros and cons of corporate partnerships. The book also addresses when to consider outsourcing, collaborating with competitors, and raising additional funds to expand the business.

Paperback   ISBN: 0-7879-6216-3

Grassroots Grants:
An Activist's Guide to Proposal Writing

FIRST EDITION

Andy Robinson

Andy Robinson describes just what it takes to win grants, including how grants fit into your complete fund raising program, using your grant proposal as an organizing plan, designing fundable projects, building your proposal piece by piece, and more.

Paperback   ISBN: 0-7879-6177-9

Inspired Philanthropy:
Your Step-by-Step Guide to Creating a Giving Plan

SECOND EDITION

Tracy Gary and Melissa Kohner

If you want to change the world, you'll want to read *Inspired Philanthropy*. No matter how much or little you have to give, you'll learn how to create a giving plan that will make your charitable giving catalytic and align it with your deepest values—to help bring about the very changes you want.

Paperback   ISBN: 0-7879-6410-7

TO ORDER, CALL **(800) 956-7739** OR VISIT US AT **www.josseybass.com/go/chardonpress**

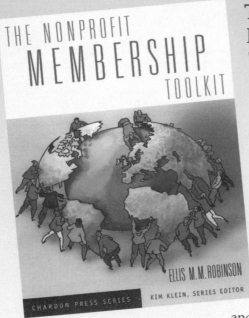